Essential English Words

WEBSTER'S WORD POWER

Essential English Words

GEDDES & GROSSET

WEBSTER'S **WORD POWER**

Morven Dooner has a masters degree in English Literature from the University of Edinburgh and is currently studying towards an MEd in Children's Literature and Literacies at the University of Glasgow. She has worked as an editor and lexicographer across many monolingual and learner dictionaries, language, reference, and education titles for HarperCollins, Chambers, Oxford University Press and Hodder and Stoughton.

Compiled By Morven Dooner
Pronunciation scheme by Scott and Bettina Montgomery

Published 2014 by Geddes & Grosset,
an imprint of The Gresham Publishing Company Ltd.,
Academy Park, Building 4000,
Gower Street, Glasgow, G51 1PR, Scotland, UK

ISBN 978-1-84205-764-3

Printed and bound in Spain by Novoprint, S.A.

This book is not published by the original publishers of
Webster's Dictionary or by their successors.

ESSENTIAL ENGLISH WORDS

Essential English Words contains around 1000 of the most commonly used words in English, as well as their inflections and word families, to help learners become natural, fluent users of the language.

Each word is listed with its parts of speech, pronunciation, inflections, and meanings.

- **parts of speech** are given in their full forms for clarity.
- **pronunciations** are given to ensure learners feel confident when speaking.
- **inflections** are given explicitly for all words.
- **definitions** give context for every word.

To aid learners with fluency, to demonstrate how to use English correctly, and to build language skills, additional help is given in the form of:

- **examples** that show learners how a word is used naturally.
- **collocations** or **word partners** are words that commonly go together and help learners get to know the word patterns that are essential for fluency and correctness in a language.
- **phrases** are common set expressions relating to the main word.
- **idioms** are figurative phrases whose words do not mean what they seem to say. Knowing common idioms is essential to understanding language.
- **common grammar patterns** that are given in examples show clearly how to use a word.
- **word families** show words that are related to or derived from the main word.
- **thesaurus** shows alternatives, so the learner doesn't overuse common words.

Grammar help is given in the following pages with:

- **irregular verbs**
- **modal verbs**
- **pronouns** and **possessives**

To further **guide** the learner and build **vocabulary**, many more additional words are given in the form of **thematic lists**.

To help perfect usage, these lists are followed by **Exercises to Help You Learn English,** a section of questions about the headwords listed in this book. Answers are provided, however, why not use the entries in the book to help you find your answers. This will help you learn.

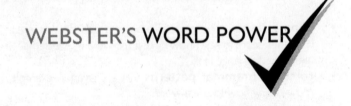

WEBSTER'S WORD POWER

CONTENTS

ESSENTIAL ENGLISH WORDS

a /a/ or **an** /an/ *indefinite article*

1 You use the word **a** when you want to say any, some, or one.
Can I have a slice of cake?

2 You use the word **a** when you want to say one single thing.
There isn't a garage for miles.

3 You use the word **a** when you want to say per or for each.
Take your medicine twice a day.

➔ *usage*
You use the word **an** before a vowel, for example **an apple, an elephant**, or **an orange**.

above /a-**buv**/ *adverb, preposition*

1 If one thing is above another thing, it is higher than or over it.
They live in a flat above the shop.
There is a picture of my grandmother above the fire.

2 If a measurement, level, or amount of something is above another measurement, level, or amount, it is greater than it.
The temperature is above average for this time of year.

➔ *collocation*
Above all, *we are delighted to be having a baby.*

abroad /a-**brawd**/ *adverb*

If you are abroad, you are in a country that is not your own.
We like to go abroad on holiday.

accent /**ac**-sent/ *noun* **accents**

1 a way certain people or groups speak, often if they are from a specific area or region
He has a distinct New York accent.

2 a mark that indicates a special emphasis given to part of a word
The accent on the e of léger is called an acute.

accept /ak-**sept**/ *verb* **accepts, accepting, accepted**

1 If you accept something that is offered, you receive it.
I accept your gift with thanks.

2 If you accept something as a fact, you regard it as true.
I will not accept his excuse.

→ *collocation*
*I **accepted** the present **from** my grandmother.*
*I **accept that** you are right about the school.*

→ *word family*
acceptable /ak-**sep**-ta-bl/ *adjective*

1 If something is acceptable, it is good enough.
His work isn't exceptional, but it is acceptable.

2 If an action or situation is acceptable, it is allowable or tolerable.
They detected acceptable levels of radiation.

access /ak-**sess**/

* *noun*
An access to something is a way to it or a means of approach.
The access to the house is hidden.

→ *usage*
The noun **access** has no plural.

✳ *verb* **accesses, accessing, accessed**

1 If you access something, you find a way to it.
   Can you access the water pipes from the kitchen?

2 If you access a computer file, you open it.
   He accessed the files on the hard drive.

➜ **word family**
   accessible /ak-**sess**-i-bl/ *adjective*

1 If someone is accessible, they are easily approached.
   He is an accessible manager.

2 If somewhere is accessible, it is easily reached.
   The villages in the mountains are not accessible.

3 If something is accessible, it is easily obtained or understood.
   The information on the website is accessible.

accommodate /a-**com**-o-date/ *verb* **accommodates, accommodating, accommodated**

1 If you accommodate a person or group of people, you provide a place for them to stay.
   As our hotel is in such a remote place, we try to accommodate all passing travellers.

2 If a building can accommodate something, it has space for it.
   The garage can accommodate three cars.

3 If you accommodate someone with something, you supply them with it.
   The bank offered to accommodate us with a loan until the mortgage was approved.

➜ **word family**
   accommodation /a-com-o-**day**-shun/ *noun*
   a place for people to stay
   Student accommodation is provided nearby.

→ *usage*

The word **accommodation** is only ever used in the singular. You should never say **accommodations**.

achieve /a-**cheev**/ *verb* **achieves, achieving, achieved**

If you achieve something, you succeed in doing it with some effort.
We have achieved what we set out to do.

→ *word family*

achievement /a-**cheev**-ment/ *noun* **achievements**
something done successfully
Opening the bakery was a great achievement.

acknowledge /ak-**naw**-ledge/ *verb* **acknowledges, acknowledging, acknowledged**

1   If you acknowledge something, you admit it is true.
He acknowledged that he was wrong.

2   If you acknowledge a letter, email, or message, you say that you have received it.
Please acknowledge receipt of this email by return.

across /a-cross/ *preposition, adverb*

from one side of something to the other
Take the boat across the river.
The bridge is across the railway.

act /act/

∗   *noun*

1   something done or carried out
It was a brave act.

2   a part of a theatrical play
The first act was a triumph.

3   a practised performance
The comedian has adapted his act for television.

* *verb* **acts, acting, acted**

1 If you act, you do something or carry something out.
If you act too hastily you can make poor choices.

2 If you act, you perform in a dramatic work.
He was acting in a play by William Shakespeare.

3 If you act, you pretend to do something.
He acted like he didn't know her.

➔ *word family*

action /**ac**-shun/ *noun*
Take action to prevent your house being burgled.

actor /**ac**-tor/ *noun*
The actor played the part superbly.

activity /ac-**ti**-vit-ee/ *noun*
To me, golf is a pointless activity.

address

* *verb* /a-**dress**/ **addressed, addressing, addressed**

1 If you address people, you speak to them.
The politician addressed the crowd.

2 If you address a letter to someone, you write
the place where they live or work on the envelope.

* *noun* /**a**-dress, a-**dress**/ **addresses**

1 the place where a person lives or works
What is your address?

2 the directions on a letter or envelope
The address on the letter is not correct.

➔ *collocations*

*I will send this to your **email address**.*
*Can you tell me your company's **web address**?*

adult /**a**-dult, a-**dult**/

* *adjective*
If a person or animal is described as an adult,

they are no longer a child, and are fully grown.
The adult bears protect their cubs fiercely.

✳ *noun* **adults**

a mature, fully grown person or animal
Will there be any adults supervising the children's party?

---

adventure /ad-**ven**-cher/ *noun* **adventures**

an exciting or dangerous deed or undertaking
We are going on an exciting adventure to the North Pole.

➔ *word family*

adventurous /ad-**ven**-che-russ/ *adjective*

1 If someone is described as adventurous, they are
daring, or eager for adventure.
The adventurous children were climbing trees.

2 If something is described as adventurous, it is
dangerous, and involves risk.
We are about to begin an adventurous journey.

---

advice /ad-**vice**/ *noun*

a helpful opinion offered by one person to another
I need to seek expert financial advice.

➔ *usage*

Remember that you should never say **an advice**.
Instead you say **any advice** or **some advice**.

---

affect /a-**fect**/ *verb* **affects, affecting, affected**

1 If you are affected by something, you are
changed, influenced, or harmed by it.
The disease has affected his eyes.

2 If something affects you, it makes you feel emotional.
My mother was deeply affected by her own father's death.

➔ *usage*

Do not confuse the words **affect** and **effect**.

afford /a-**ford**/ verb **affords, affording, afforded**

1   If you can afford something, you are able to pay for it.
     They can afford to go on holiday this year.

2   If you can afford to do something, you are able to do it without trouble or loss.
     I can't afford the time at the moment.

➔   *collocation*
     *I can't **afford to go** to the cinema this week.*

afraid /a-**frade**/ adjective

If someone is afraid of something, they are frightened of it.
I am afraid of the dark, and sleep with the light on.

➔   *collocation*
     *I am **afraid to go** outside at night.*

age /**ayj**/

✱   *noun* **ages**
how old someone or something is
He guessed the age of the boy to be 15.

✱   *verb* **ages, ageing, aged**
If you age, you grow old or look older. If you age something, you work out how old it is.

agree /a-**gree**/ verb agrees, agreeing, agreed

If you agree with someone, you share the same opinion.
I agree with you that spinach is horrible.

ahead /a-**hed**/ adverb

If something is ahead, it is in front.
Please go on ahead to clear the way.

➔   *phrase*
If you **look** or **plan ahead**, you plan for the future.
You need to plan ahead for the whole project.

aim /aim/

✻ *verb* **aims, aiming, aimed**

1 If you aim a weapon at someone or something, you point it at them.
   He aimed the arrow at the target.

2 If you aim to do something, you intend or try to do it.
   I aim to win this competition.

✻ *noun* **aims**

1 the act of aiming a weapon
   Your aim needs to improve, as you are missing the target.

2 an intention, goal, or purpose
   Our aim is to win this game.

alcohol /**al**-ku-hol/ *noun*

a drink such as beer or wine that can make you drunk
   My religion does not allow me to drink alcohol.

➜ *usage*
   The word **alcohol** has no plural.

allow /al-**ow**/ *verb* **allows, allowing, allowed**

If you allow something, you permit it.
   The children are not allowed to watch TV during the day.

➜ *usage*
   Do not say **it is not allowed to do something.**
   Instead say **I am/you are/they are not allowed to do something** or **something is not allowed.**

along /**a**-long/ *preposition, adverb*

1 from one part of something to another
   Please move along the corridor to the hall.

2 forwards
   The bus moved slowly along the road.

aloud /a-**loud**/ adverb

If you say, laugh, or read something aloud, you do so in order that it can be heard.
I read aloud to the children every evening.

already /ol-**red**-ee/ adverb

1 If something has been done already, it has been done before this present time.
I have already seen the movie.
2 If you say that something is happening or has happened already, it is doing so now, or has done so before the expected time.
Are you leaving already?
Did you get milk already?

also /**ol**-so/ adverb

in addition
We are also going to the party on Saturday.

altogether /ol-te-**ge**-ther/ adverb

1 wholly or completely
I am not altogether satisfied with the service in this hotel.
2 including everything
The lunch is £20 altogether.
➔ *collocation*
*I'm not **altogether pleased** about this situation.*

always /**ol**-waze/ adverb

If you always do something, you do it at all times, or most of the time.
I always go swimming on Tuesday afternoons.
➔ *collocation*
*That was an amazing meal, **as always.***

amaze /a-**maze**/ verb amazes, amazing, amazed

If someone is amazed by something, they are surprised by it.

Her rudeness amazed me.

amount /a-**mount**/

* verb **amounts, amounting, amounted**

If something amounts to a number, it adds up to it.

The bill amounts to £300.

* noun **amounts**

an amount of something is how much there is of it

There is a small amount of food in the fridge.

➔ **usage**

Remember, you can put 'large' and 'small' in front of the noun **amount**, but not 'big' or 'little'.

amuse /a-**myooz**/ verb amuses, amusing, amused

If you are amused by something, it entertains you or gives you pleasure.

The children were most amused by the story.

and /and/ conjunction

1   You use the word **and** to say as well as.

I would like ice cream and jelly.

He bought eggs, milk, bread and butter.

2   You use the word **and** to join parts of a sentence together.

We went to the park and then we went swimming.

I went to a party and Sue was wearing the same dress.

anger /**ang**-ger/

✻ *noun*

a strong feeling of rage or fury

I felt anger at my brother's behaviour.

✻ *verb* **angers, angering, angered**

If something angers you, it makes you feel rage or fury.

His rude behaviour angered me.

➔ *usage*

The noun **anger** has no plural.

➔ *word family*

angry /**ang**-gree/ *adjective*

If you are angry, you feel rage and fury.

I am so angry about the recent price rises.

animal /a-ni-mal/ *noun* **animals**

1 a living being with the power to feel and move at will

A lion is a wild animal.

2 a living being other than a human being

We care about animals as well as people.

announce /a-**nounse**/ *verb* **announces, announcing, announced**

If you announce something, you make it known.

They have announced their engagement.

➔ *word family*

announcement /a-**nounse**-ment/ *noun*

a statement about something that is about to happen

We were delighted to hear the announcement of your promotion.

annoy /an-**noy**/ *verb* **annoys, annoying, annoyed**
If something annoys you, you are troubled by it.
The sound of the car alarm annoyed me all night.

➔ *word family*
annoyance /an-**noy**-ans/ *noun* **annoyances**
something that troubles you
Much to my annoyance, my brother was late for dinner.

another /an-**noth**-er/ *determiner, pronoun*
1 one more person or thing
   I would like another sandwich.
2 a person besides yourself
   Stealing is taking another's property.

answer /an-ser/
* *verb* **answers, answering, answered**
   If you answer something, you reply to it.
   I answered her letter on Friday.
* *noun* **answers**
   a reply
   Have you had an answer to your question?
➔ *usage*
   Remember that the preposition **to** is used with the noun **answer**.

appear /a-**peer**/ *verb* **appears, appearing, appeared**
1 If something appears, it comes into sight.
   The castle appeared out of the mist.
2 If something appears to be something, it seems to be so.
   She appears to be sad.

→ *collocation*
I **appear to** be working this weekend.

apple /a-pl/ *noun* **apples**

a sweet green or red fruit with a hard skin

→ *idiom*
If someone is the **apple of your eye**, you think very highly of them.

apply /a-**ply**/ *verb* **applies, applying, applied**

1 If you apply something, you put or spread it on.
Apply the ointment to the wound.

2 If you apply force, you use force.
Apply force to the wound.

3 If you apply yourself to something, you pay attention or concentrate on it.
Apply yourself to your work.

arm /arm/ *noun* **arms**

1 one of the upper limbs, the part of the body from the shoulder to the hand
I broke my left arm when I fell off my bike.

2 The arm of a piece of furniture is the place where you rest your arms.
She put her cup on the arm of the chair.

→ *phrase*
If you walk **arm in arm** with someone, you hold their arm.

arrange /a-**range**/ *verb* **arranges, arranging, arranged**

1 If you arrange something, you put it into order.
I have arranged the books on the shelves.

2 If you arrange to do something, you make plans or preparations.
I'd like to arrange a meeting for Tuesday afternoon.

arrive /a-**rive**/ *verb* **arrives, arriving, arrived**

1 When something arrives, it comes.
The day of the wedding arrived.
2 If you arrive at a place, you reach it after a journey.
I was delighted when we eventually arrived home.
→ *usage*
Remember to use the preposition **in** with the verb **arrive**.

art /art/ *noun* **arts**

1 a particular ability or skill
She is practised in the art of conversation.
2 the practice of painting, sculpture, and architecture, etc
She is studying art at college.
3 examples of painting, sculpture, etc
The gallery is showing modern art.

aside /a-**side**/ *adverb*

1 If you put something aside, you put it on one side.
She put some money aside every week for a holiday.
2 If you take someone aside, you take them to one side.
I took her aside to tell her the secret.
→ *collocation*
*Please **stand aside** to let the doctor see the patient.*

ask /ask/ verb asks, asking, asked

1 If you ask someone for something, you request it of them.
   Could you ask that man for directions?

2 If you ask someone about something, you inquire it of them.
   Have you asked the other children how old they are?

→ *usage*
   Remember that you **ask** someone something, or **ask** something **of** someone. You don't ask something **to** someone.

asleep /a-**sleep**/ adjective, adverb

If you are asleep, you are sleeping.
I remained asleep despite the noise of the car alarm.

→ *phrase*
   If you **fall asleep**, you start sleeping.

attach /a-tach/ verb attaches, attaching, attached

If you attach something to something else you join them together.
Attach the rope to the boat.

→ *phrase*
   If you are **attached to** something you are fond of it.

attract /a-**tract**/ verb attracts, attracting, attracted

1 If someone or something attracts you, they have qualities which you like or desire.
   I am attracted to funny people.

2 If someone or something attracts attention, it gets attention.
   I tried to attract my aunt's attention.

aware /a-**ware**/ *adjective*

> If you are aware of a situation, you have
> knowledge of it.
> *I am aware of the difficulties.*

away /**a**-way/ *adverb*

1 to or in a different place
   I am moving away from the village.
2 at a distance
➜ *collocation*
   *Does your Gran live **far away**?*

awful /**aw**-ful/ *adjective*

> If something is awful, it is very bad or unpleasant.
> *There was an awful accident in town last week.*

baby /**bay**-bee/ *noun*

> the young of a person or animal
> *Our baby is nine months old.*

back /back/

✻ *noun* **backs**
1 the part of the body from the bottom of the neck
   to the base of the spine
2 the rear part of something
✻ *verb* **backs, backing, backed**
1 If you back somewhere, you go in the opposite
   way from the way you are facing.
➜ *collocation*
   *I **backed out** of the garage.*
2 If you back someone or something, you support
   them or it.
   We backed the plans for expansion.

➔ *phrases*

If you **back away from** something, you move away.
If you **back down from** something, you stop doing it.
If you **back off** from something, you move away from it to prevent anything bad from happening.
If you **back** someone **up**, you support them.

bad /bad/ *adjective* **worse, worst**

1   If something is bad, it is unpleasant or harmful.
I was worried because your flu seemed so bad.

2   If the standard of something is bad, it is not good.
Your work has been very bad lately.

3   If a person is bad, they are naughty or mischievous.
He was sent to his bedroom for being bad.

4   A bad mistake is a serious one.
He had made a very bad mistake in his application for the job.

5   If food goes bad, it is rotten or spoiled.
The meat had to be thrown away because it had gone bad.

6   If someone feels bad about something, they are sorry or apologetic.
She feels bad about not going to the party.

➔ *phrases*

If you say something is **not bad**, you mean that it is satisfactory.
If you are **bad at** something, you cannot do it well.
If something is **bad for you**, it can cause you harm.

→ *word family*
badly *adverb*

1 If someone does something badly, they do not do it well.
She did badly in her exams.

2 If someone is badly injured, they are seriously injured.

3 If something is badly damaged, it is seriously damaged.

4 If someone wants or needs something badly, they want or need it very much.

→ *usage*
Remember that the word **bad** is always used as an adjective and never as an adverb. If you want to describe how someone has done something, use the adverb **badly**.

balance /**ba**-lanse/

* *noun* **balances**

1 equality of power
The major countries of the world are trying to achieve a balance of power.

2 a state of physical steadiness
I lost my balance and fell over.

* *verb* **balances, balancing, balanced**

1 If you balance something, or it is balanced, it is made equal.
Can we balance the numbers of women and men in government?

2 If you balance on something, you keep steady or upright on top of it.
The acrobats were balancing on a tightrope.

ball /**bawl**/ *noun* **balls**

1   anything round in shape
    I bought a ball of wool for knitting.
2   a round or roundish object used in games
➜   *collocations*
    a tennis ball
    a football
3   a rounded part of something
    I balanced on the ball of my foot.
4   a formal social event involving dancing
➜   *phrase*
    If you **have a ball**, you have a really good time.

band /**band**/

∗   *noun* **bands**
1   anything used to bind or tie together
    She tied her hair back with a band.
2   a group of people united for a purpose, especially
    to play music together
    I'm going to see my favourite band tonight.
∗   *verb* **bands, banding, banded**
    If people band together, they come together to try
    to achieve something they all want.
    The community have banded together to fight crime.

bank /**bangk**/

∗   *noun* **banks**
1   a place where money is put for safekeeping
    I must go to the bank to pay a cheque in.
2   a ridge or mound of earth, etc
    I climbed onto a grassy bank.
3   the ground at the side of a river, lake, etc
    The bank at the lake is rather slippy.

✳ *verb* **banks, banking, banked**

1 If you bank money, you put it into a bank.
I banked the cheque on Thursday.

2 If something is banked, it is piled in heaps.
Snow banked up at the sides of the road.

➜ *phrase*
If you are **banking on** something you are relying on it for success.
I'm banking on you to support me.

➜ *word family*
banker /**bang**-ker/ *noun*
someone who runs or manages a bank
banking /**bang**-king/ *noun*
the business of a banker

bar /**bar**/

✳ *noun* **bars**

1 a solid piece of something, such as wood, metal, chocolate, or soap, that is longer than it is wide
I ate a bar of chocolate.

2 a length of wood or metal across a door or window to keep it shut or prevent entrance through it
There are iron bars across the windows.

3 a counter at which food or drink may be bought and consumed
I'm going to the sandwich bar at lunchtime.

4 a place where alcoholic drinks are served
I'll meet you at the bar for a drink at 7 pm.

✳ *verb* **bars, barring, barred**

1 If someone bars a door or a window, they lock it by placing a bar across it.

2   If someone is barred from doing something, they are prevented from doing it.
→   *collocation*
    We **were barred from** entering the library.

basis /**base**-iss/ *noun* **bases** /**base**-eez/
___
something on which another thing is built up, the foundation or beginning
Your argument has a firm basis.

bath /**bath**/ *noun* **baths**
___
a large vessel in which the body is washed
I prefer to wash in the bath rather than take a shower.
→   *collocation*
    I always **take a bath** on Sundays.

be /**bee**/ *verb* **am, are, is; was, were; being; been**
___
1   To be is to exist or live in a certain place. If you are somewhere you exist in that place.
    He is on holiday in Rome.
2   To be is to exist or live in a certain state or way, or to be doing a certain thing.
    I was embarrassed by my mistake last week.
    The boy is running.
3   If you are something you are the same as that thing.
    I am a gardener.
4   You can show a sense of time by saying it is.
    It is 4 o'clock.
    Our anniversary was last Wednesday.

beach /**beech**/ *noun* **beaches**
___
the shore of a sea or lake, often covered in sand

bear[1] /bare/ *verb* **bears, bearing, bore, borne**

1   If you bear something, such as pain, you put up with it.
    I could no longer bear the pain in my tooth.
2   If something bears something else, it supports it.
    The chair can bear his weight.
3   If you bear something, such as a mark, you have it or you show it.
    I'm still bearing a scar from my accident.
4   If you bear in a given direction, you move towards it.
    Can you bear left now please?

bear[2] /bare/ *noun* **bears**

a wild animal with thick fur and sharp claws

beat /beet/

*   *verb* **beats, beating, beat, beaten**
1   If you beat something, you hit it several times.
    I was beating my hand against the drum.
→   ***thesaurus***
    hit, pound, punch
2   If a person or team beats another person or team, they defeat them.
    The home team beat the visiting team in the match.
3   If you beat something, such as a cake mixture, you mix it vigorously with a fork or a whisk.
    Beat the eggs and the sugar together, then add the flour.
*   *noun* **beats**
    a regular rhythm
    the beat of the drum.

bed /bed/ *noun* **beds**

1   a thing to sleep or rest on
    I go to bed at 10 o'clock every night.

2 the channel of a river

After five weeks of no rain, the river bed was dry.

3 a piece of ground prepared for growing flowers
and plants

I would like to dig a new flower bed in the garden.

---

begin /bi-**gin**/ *verb* **begins, beginning, began, begun**

1 If you begin something, you start to do it.

He began to play the piano.

2 If you begin something, you are the first to do it.

Would you like to begin the discussion?

➔ *thesaurus*

start, establish, initiate, lead

➔ *word family*

beginner /bi-**gi**-ner/ *noun* **beginners**

someone starting to learn something

She has started going to a beginner's dance class.

beginning /bi-**gin**-ing/ *noun* **beginnings**

the start of something

The beginning of the story is quite dull but it improves.

---

behind /bee-**hind**/ *preposition*

at the back of something or someone

I was behind the house.

---

belief /be-**leef**/ *noun* **beliefs**

1 a faith in something, such as a religion

I have a belief in God.

2 a trust in something

The incident shook her belief in his ability.

3 an opinion about something

It is my belief that she is guilty.

believe /be-**leeve**/ verb believes, believing, believed

1 If you believe that something exists, you accept it is true or real.
   I believe in ghosts.
2 If you believe in something such as a law or power, you have trust in it.
   I believe in the power of the law.
3 If you believe in a god, you have faith in that god.
   I believe in God.
➔ *word family*
   believable /be-**lee**-va-bul/ *adjective*
   making you accept something is true or real
   His story is believable.

belong /bi-**long**/ verb belongs, belonging, belonged

1 If something belongs to you, it is your property.
   That bike belongs to me.
2 If you belong to a place or club, you are a member of it.
   I belong to the health club at the local hotel.
3 If you belong to a town, city, or area, you are connected to it.
   I belong to New York, although I'm originally from London.
➔ *word family*
   belongings /bi-**long**-ing-z/ *plural noun*
   the things that are one's own property
   I took my belongings away with me.

beneath /bi-**neeth**/ preposition

under or at a lower level than
The dog lay beneath the table.

beside /bi-**side**/ *preposition*

next to

I was sitting beside my sister.

➔ *idiom*

If you are **beside yourself with worry or anger**, you are very intensely worried or angry.

bet /**bet**/

* *noun* **bets**

money put down in support of an opinion, to be either lost or returned with interest

* *verb* **bets, betting, bet**

If you bet on something, you stake money on it.

➔ *collocation*

*My father regularly **puts a bet on** the horses.*

between /bi-**tween**/ *preposition*

1 at or in the space, time, etc, separating two things

I had five minutes between meetings to take the call.

2 connecting from one thing to another

There is a very close bond between the two brothers.

beyond /bi-**yond**/

* *preposition*

on the farther side of something

The school was built beyond the park.

* *adverb*

at a distance

The sky beyond was dark with clouds.

bill /**bill**/ *noun* **bills**

a written statement for money that you owe for goods or services

At the end of the meal we asked the waiter for the bill.

→ *collocations*
  electricity bill
  phone bill
  gas bill

bird /bird/ noun **birds**
a creature with feathers and wings that usually flies

bite /bite/
* *verb* **bites, biting, bit, bitten**
If you bite something or someone, you cut or pierce it or them with your teeth.
I bit the apple hungrily.

* *noun* **bites**
1 the amount bitten off something
→ *collocation*
  *She took a **bite out of** the apple.*
2 the wound made by biting
  The man showed us his shark bite.

bitter /bit-ter/ adjective
1 sharp to the taste
  Lemons are much more bitter than oranges.
2 severe or piercing
  This cold weather is bitter.
3 painful
  She had learned from bitter experience.
4 feeling or showing hatred, hostility, envy, or disappointment
  She was feeling bitter about her divorce.
→ *word family*
  bitterly *adverb*
  very much, in a bad way

➔ *collocation*
It was **bitterly cold**.

➔ *word family*
bitterness *noun*
the state of feeling bitter

---

blood /blud/ *noun*

the red liquid in the bodies of people and animals
There was blood all over her hand after she accidentally cut her finger with a knife.

➔ *collocation*
*We have been asked to **donate blood**.*

---

board /bored/

✳ *noun* **boards**
1 a long, broad strip of wood
My brother and I nailed boards together to make a raft.
2 food
I have asked for board as well as lodgings.
3 a group of people who meet, for example, for business reasons
I have a meeting with the board of directors.

✳ *verb* **boards, boarding, boarded**
1 If you board up something such as a window or door, you cover it with boards.
We boarded the broken windows up after the storm.
2 If you board somewhere, you get to live there and get your food supplied.
The pupils board at the school during term time.
3 If you board a bus or a train, you get onto it.
I need to board the bus at midday.

boat /**bote**/ *noun* **boats**

1   a ship, especially a small one
I went sailing in a boat last week.

2   a dish shaped like a boat
We always serve gravy in a gravy boat.

➔   *idiom*
If you are in the **same boat as someone**, you are in a similar situation to them.

body /**bod**-ee/ *noun* **bodies**

1   the physical structure of a human being or animal
My entire body hurts after my exercise class.

2   the main part of anything
The body of the text is in a different font to the rest of the book.

3   a group of people
There was a troublemaker among the body of spectators.

4   a dead body
Police are looking for a body.

bone /**bone**/ *noun* **bones**

the hard substance forming the skeleton of human beings and animals
We are all made of flesh and bone.

book /**book**/

✳   *noun*
a piece of writing several hundred pages long
Read the book from cover to cover.

✳   *verb* **books, booking, booked**
If you book something, you reserve it.
Book a place for me on the trip.

border /**bor**-der/

✳ *noun* **borders**

1 the outer edge of anything
   There is a white border round the picture.

2 the boundary between two countries
   I was asked to show my passport at the border.

✳ *verb* **borders, bordering, bordered**
   If something borders something else, it is next to it.
   The farm bordering ours is for sale.

➔ *phrase*
   If something **borders on** something, it comes close to it.

borrow /**bor**-o/ *verb* **borrows, borrowing, borrowed**
   If you borrow something, you ask or receive it as a loan.
   I had to borrow money from the bank.
   I borrowed a book from the library.

➔ *word family*
   borrower /**bor**-o-wer/ *noun*
   someone who borrows something

both /**bothe**/ *pronoun*
   something that is true for the two people or things referred to
   We are both looking for new jobs.

➔ *collocation*
   *I would like to take **both of you** to the park.*

bottle /**baw**-tl/

✳ *noun* **bottles**
   a container, usually of glass, with a narrow neck

bowl

* *verb* **bottles, bottling, bottled**
  If you bottle something, you put it into bottles.
  They bottle wine at the vineyard.
➔ *phrase*
  If you **bottle up** your feelings, you don't show them.

bowl /bole/ *noun* **bowls**
  a roundish dish or basin
  I served pudding in a bowl.

box¹ /boks/
* *noun* **boxes**
  a case or container
  There were ten boxes of books to unpack.
* *verb* **boxes, boxing, boxed**
  If you box something, you put it in a box.
  I boxed all of our belongings before we moved house.

box² /boks/ *verb* **boxes, boxing, boxed**
  If you box as a sport, you fight while wearing padded gloves.
➔ *word family*
  boxer /bok-ser/ *noun* **boxers**
  someone who boxes as a sport

boy /boy/ *noun* **boys**
1 a male child
  My sister has three children: two boys and a girl.
2 a young male person
  There are as many boys as girls on the football team.

→ **word family**
boyhood /**boy**-hood/ *noun*
the period during which a male person is a child

boyfriend /**boy**-frend/ *noun* **boyfriends**
a man or boy with whom you are in a romantic
relationship

brain /**brane**/ *noun* **brains**
the soft matter within the skull, the centre of the
nervous system
She had to have an operation on her brain.

→ **word family**
brainy /**bray**-nee/ *adjective*
intelligent

bread /**bred**/ *noun* **breads**
a food made from flour or meal and baked
I made a sandwich with some bread and cheese.

break /**brake**/
✱ *verb* **breaks, breaking, broke, broken**
1 If you break something, it separates into two or
more parts.
I broke the glass vase.
2 If something breaks, it becomes unusable or in
need of repair.
If the TV breaks then it will be your fault.
3 If you break something such as a rule, promise,
or law, you fail to keep it.
In most cultures, stealing is breaking the law.

4 If you **break** something such as news to someone, you tell them it.

I had to break the news of the death to my brother.

✳ *noun* **breaks**

1 a separation, a fracture

There is a break in one of the stones in the wall.

The break in his ankle bone was very bad.

2 a pause

There will be a break halfway through the show.

➔ *word family*

breakable /**brake**-a-bul/ *adjective*

used to describe something that is easily broken

---

breakfast /**brek**-fast/ *noun* **breakfasts**

the first meal of the day

I have cereal for breakfast every morning.

---

breath /**breth**/ *noun* **breaths**

the air that you take into your lungs

➔ *collocation*

Take **a deep breath** and relax.

➔ *idiom*

If something is **a breath of fresh air**, it is refreshingly new and different.

---

breathe /**breeth**/ *verb* **breathes, breathing, breathed**

If you breathe, you take air into your lungs.

➔ *phrases*

If you **breathe in**, you take air into your lungs.

If you **breathe out**, you push air out of your lungs.

➔ *usage*

Remember that **breath** is the noun, and **breathe** is the verb.

bridge /bridge/

* *noun* **bridges**
a roadway built across a river, etc
The bridge is closed because the river has flooded.

* *verb* **bridges, bridging, bridged**
If you bridge something you create a connection that was not previously there.
Can we bridge our differences?

brief /breef/

* *adjective* **briefer, briefest**
short
He gave a brief statement to the police.

* *verb* **briefs, briefing, briefed**
If you brief someone about something, you provide them with a summary of the facts.

➔ *collocation*
*My boss **briefed me on** the meeting with the client on the way back to the office.*

bright /brite/ *adjective* **brighter, brightest**

1 used to describe something that is light or shining
There was a bright star shining in the sky.

2 strong or vivid
She was wearing a bright red lipstick.

3 clever
She is a very bright pupil.

➔ *word family*
brightness /brite-ness/ *noun*
the lightness that is produced by something that is bright

bring /bring/ verb brings, bringing, brought /brawt/

If you bring something somewhere, you fetch or carry it.

Can you bring food to the party?

➔ *phrases*

If you **bring about** something, you cause it to happen.

If you **bring** something **off**, you succeed.

If you **bring** someone **up**, you rear or educate them.

If you **bring** something **up**, you talk about it in a conversation.

brother /bru-ther/ noun brothers

a son of the same parents

My brother is six years younger than me.

budget /bu-jet/

✳ *noun* **budgets**

a plan to ensure that household expenses or those of a firm or organization will not be greater than the income available

In this time of austerity, we must keep within our monthly budget.

✳ *verb* **budgets, budgeting, budgeted**

If you budget, you make a plan to ensure your expenses are not greater than your income.

I try to budget but I always seem to spend too much.

bunch /bunch/ noun bunches

1   a group or collection of things of the same kind

➔ *phrases*
a bunch of flowers
a bunch of bananas
a bunch of keys

2 a group of people
Her friends are a very nice bunch.

burst /burst/

✻ *verb* **bursts, bursting, burst**

1 If something bursts, it breaks into pieces.
The balloon burst when it was pierced with a needle.

2 If you burst into a place, you rush, or go suddenly or violently into it.
She burst into the room.

✻ *noun* **bursts**
a sudden outbreak
There was a burst of applause when she came on stage.

bush /boosh/ *noun* **bushes**

a small low tree
We have planted fruit bushes in the garden.

business /biz-nez/ *noun* **businesses**

1 the act of buying and selling

➔ *phrase*
If you are **on business**, you are working.

➔ *usage*
Remember that you **go on business** and not **for business**.

2 a person's affairs and concerns
It is my business whether I take the job or not.

busy /**bi**-zee/ *adjective* **busier, busiest**

1   always doing something
    She was too busy to visit her family.
2   at work, engaged in a job, etc
    My dad's busy just now, but he will call you back.
3   full of people, traffic, etc
    The shops are really busy today.

→   *word family*
    busily /**bi**-zi-lee/ *adverb*
    in a busy or active way

butter /**but**-er/ *noun* **butters**

a fatty food made from milk
I spread butter on some bread.

bye /**bye**/ *interjection*

an informal way of saying goodbye

calculate /**cal**-kyu-late/ *verb* **calculates, calculating, calculated**

1   If you calculate something with numbers
    and mathematics, you work out an amount.
    Can you calculate the sums on the page?
2   If you calculate something, such as a cost,
    you use all the facts you have to make an
    estimate.
    *I asked the builder to calculate the cost of the repair
    work.*

→   *word family*
    calculating /**cal**-kyu-late-ing/ *adjective*
    scheming, clever, or sly, especially in a selfish way
    calculation /cal-kyu-**lay**-shun/ *noun*

1 the act or process of calculating

Can you make a calculation of the cost?

2 a sum

I made a mistake in the calculation.

calculator *noun*

a small electronic machine used to make mathematical calculations

---

call /cawl/

✳ *verb* **calls, calling, called**

1 If you call someone something, you describe them in a certain way.

I called my brother a thief for stealing my book.

2 If you call someone a name, you give them that name.

They called their daughter, Amy.

3 If you call someone by phone, you dial their number to speak to them.

I called my grandmother yesterday.

4 If you call someone to you, you ask them to come.

I called my friends over.

5 If you call on someone, you make a short visit.

She called on her mother on her way home from work.

➔ *usage*

Remember that you **call to someone** to ask them to come, but you **call someone on** the phone.

✳ *noun* **calls**

1 a cry

He heard a call for help.

2 a short visit

I made a call on my mother on the way home from work.

3 a telephone call
I just need to make a quick call to my husband.

4 need, demand
There is no call for that brand of coffee in this café.

→ *phrase*

If something is a **close call**, something bad very nearly happens.

If you **call something off**, you stop it or cancel it.

---

calm /**cahm**/
___

* *adjective* **calmer, calmest**

1 quiet, still
It was a calm day without any wind at all.

2 unexcited, not agitated
We remained calm during the bomb alert.

* *noun*

1 stillness
There was calm after the storm.

2 freedom from excitement
I admired her calm during the bomb scare.

* *verb* **calms, calming, calmed**

If you calm someone, you make them calm.
I calmed my brother after the fight.

If you calm down, you stop being anxious or afraid.

→ *collocation*

*My sister **calmed me down** after the bomb scare.*

→ *word family*

calmness /**cahm**-ness/ *noun*

the quality of being calm
There was a great calmness after the storm.

camera /**ca**-me-ra/ *noun* **cameras**

a device for taking photographs or recording images

→ *collocation*

*He has a new **digital camera**.*

can /**can**/ *verb* **could**

1 If you can do something, you are able to do it.
I can jump really high.

2 If you ask if you can do something, you ask to be allowed to do it.
Can I have a cake?

3 If you ask if someone can do something, you ask them to do it.
Can you drive me to the park?

→ *usage*

You say **cannot** or **can't** as the negative of **can**.
I can't go out tonight.

cap /**cap**/

✳ *noun* **caps**

1 a hat for the head with no brim, or only part of one
I wear a baseball cap when I go running.

2 a cover or lid
I asked my friend to open the cap of the bottle.

✳ *verb* **caps, capping, capped**

1 If you cap something, you put a lid on it.
Could you cap the bottle please?

2 If something is capped, it is improved on.
In order to win, he must cap his opponent's performance.

3 If an amount is capped, it has a limit put on it.
There is a cap on my broadband usage.

capital /**ca**-pi-tal/

✽ *adjective*

If something such as a city is described as capital, it is the most important of its kind.

London is the capital city of the United Kingdom.

✽ *noun* **capitals**

1 the chief city of a country or area

Nashville is the capital of the state of Tennessee.

2 money, especially when used for business

We have no money this month, so will need to borrow capital from the bank.

3 a large letter, as used first in proper names

Charlotte is spelt with a capital C at the beginning.

car /**car**/ *noun* **cars**

a vehicle with four wheels and seating for around four people

I drove the car to the supermarket.

carry /**ca**-ree/ *verb* **carries, carrying, carried**

1 If you carry something from one place to the other, you take it there.

Could you please carry the chairs from the van to the hall.

2 If something is carried, it goes from one place to another.

The sound of his voice carried to the next room.

3 If you carry something, you have or hold it.

The job carries great responsibility.

The lorry can carry a whole range of goods.

→ *phrases*

If you **carry on** with something, you continue to do it.

If you **carry on,** you behave badly or in an uncontrolled manner.

If you **carry** something **out,** you perform it.

---

cat /cat/ *noun* **cats**

an animal with soft fur and sharp claws, commonly kept as a pet

My mother keeps three cats in her house.

---

category /ca-te-go-ree/ *noun* **categories**

a class or group of things in a system of grouping

There are many categories of books in the library, including fiction, non-fiction, and reference.

---

cause /cawz/

∗ *noun* **causes**

1 something or someone that produces an effect or result

➔ *collocations*

*An electrical fault was **the cause of** the fire.*

*He was **the cause of** his father's unhappiness.*

2 the reason for an action

➔ *collocations*

*There was **no cause** to treat her so badly.*

*We have **little cause** for complaint.*

3 a purpose or aim

It was done in the cause of peace.

∗ *verb* **causes, causing, caused**

If you cause something to happen, you make it so.

The accident was caused by the pedestrian running across the road.

celebrate /**se**-le-brate/ *verb* **celebrates, celebrating, celebrated**

If you celebrate an event, you do something special for it, such as holding a party or a formal dinner.
We held a party to celebrate her birthday.

➔ *word family*
celebration /se-le-**bray**-shon/ *noun*
a party to mark a special event
celebrated /**se**-le-bray-ted/ *adjective*
famous
She is a celebrated artist.

centre /**sen**-ter/

* *noun* **centres**
1 the middle point or part of anything
The centre of the circle.
I drove to the centre of town.
2 a place where certain activities or facilities are concentrated
There is a great book shop in the shopping centre.
* *verb* **centres, centring, centred**
If you centre something, you put it into the middle.
I centred the picture on the wall.

ceremony /**se**-re-mo-nee/ *noun* **ceremonies**

the performing of certain actions in a fixed order for a religious or other serious purpose
The wedding ceremony was held in the local church.

→ *word family*
ceremonial /se-re-**moe**-nee-al/

∗ *noun* **ceremonials**
the actions connected with a ceremony

∗ *adjective*
having to do with a ceremony
ceremonious /se-re-**moe**-nee-es/ *adjective*
full of ceremony, very formal

---

chain /**chane**/

∗ *noun* **chains**
1 a number of metal rings joined to form a rope
The poor dog was fastened to the fence by a chain.
She wore a silver chain around her neck.
2 a number of connected facts or events
The accident was caused by a strange chain of events.

∗ *verb* **chains, chaining, chained**
If you chain something, you bind or fasten it with a chain.
I chained my bike to the fence.

---

chair /**chair**/

∗ *noun* **chairs**
1 a moveable seat with a back
I sit on a high-backed chair when working.
2 a person who is in charge of a meeting
The chair started proceedings at the meeting.

∗ *verb* **chairs, chairing, chaired**
If you chair a meeting, you are in charge of it.
I am chairing the annual general meeting.

challenge /**cha**-lenj/
✻ *verb* **challenges, challenging, challenged**
1 If you challenge someone, you call on them to fight or play a match to see which of you is better.
   I challenged my brother to a game of darts.
2 If you challenge something, you voice your doubt of the truth of it.
   I challenged his statement that the substance was safe.
✻ *noun* **challenges**
1 the daring of another to a contest
   I accept your challenge to a game of darts.
2 a statement or action that questions something
   It was seen as a challenge to the leader's authority.
3 a difficult or exciting task
   My new job is a challenge.
➔ *word family*
   challenger *noun*
   someone or something that challenges someone or something else

change /**chanje**/
✻ *verb* **changes, changing, changed**
1 If you change, or are changed by something, you become different.
   Her lifestyle has changed since her health scare.
   The wind changed direction.
2 If you change something, you make it different.
   I changed my mind after reading the article.
   Please change your clothes before we go out.
3 If you change one thing for another, you put one thing in the other's place.
   I need to change my library books.

* *noun* **changes**
1 a difference or alteration
 I see a change in her since her time abroad.
2 money given back for too much money received
 I was given the wrong change by the shop assistant.
→ **word family**
 changeable *adjective*
 used to describe something or someone liable to change

charge /charj/

* *verb* **charges, charging, charged**
1 If you charge for something, you ask a price for it.
 I felt the shopkeeper charged me too much for the mirror.
2 If you charge someone with something, you accuse them of it.
 He was charged with murdering his brother.
3 If you charge at or into something, you rush at or into it.
 The children came charging into the room.
4 If you charge something such as a battery, a computer, or a mobile phone, you fill it with electricity or energy.
 I need to charge my phone before we go out.
* *noun* **charges**
1 custody or guardianship
 The child was put in her father's charge.
2 a price
 The hotel's charges are very expensive.
3 an accusation
 The man was faced with a charge of murder.

→ *phrases*

If you **take charge**, you take command or control.
If you are **in charge**, you are in control of people or a situation.

charity /cha-ri-tee/ *noun* charities

1 an organization that raises money to help people in need or other causes
   I'm collecting money in aid of a children's charity.
2 (no plural) the quality of being kind and giving to other people
   She shows great charity to her elderly neighbours.

→ *word family*

charitable /cha-ri-ta-bl/ *adjective*
used to describe someone who shows charity

cheap /cheep/ *adjective* cheaper, cheapest

1 If something is cheap, it is of a low price.
   The cakes in this shop are the cheapest in town.
2 If something is cheap, it is of little value.
   His clothes look very cheap and badly made.

cheat /cheet/

* *verb* cheats, cheating, cheated
   If you cheat at a game or an exam, you deceive or use unfair means to win or do well.
   My brother always cheats at cards.

→ *collocation*
   *I was **cheated out of** my money.*

* *noun* cheats
   a person who cheats
   He is such a cheat at cards!

cheer /cheer/

* *noun* **cheers**
a shout of joy or encouragement
The cheers of the football supporters could be heard all over the town.

* *verb* **cheers, cheering, cheered**
If you cheer or cheer on someone, you encourage them, especially by shouting.
The fans were cheering on their football team.

→ *phrases*
If you **cheer up,** or if you **cheer someone up**, you brighten up or make them brighten up.

→ *word family*
cheerful /cheer-ful/ *adjective*
1 happy and lively
→ *collocations*
a cheerful person
a cheerful mood
2 bright and attractive
She always wears cheerful colours.
cheerless /cheer-less/ *adjective*
sad, gloomy
She led me into a cheerless room.

cheese /cheez/ *noun* **cheeses**
a solid food made from milk
We had bread and cheese with soup for lunch.

chest /chest/ *noun* **chests**
1 a large, strong box
I packed several chests when we moved from the UK.

2 the front, upper part of the body, from the
shoulders to the lowest ribs
He developed a chest infection after being out in the cold.

chew /choo/ *verb* **chews, chewing, chewed**

If you chew something, you crush it with your teeth.
His tooth was so sore he could hardly chew his food.

➔ *idiom*

If you **chew something over**, you discuss it with
someone or think it over.

chief /cheef/

✳ *adjective*
1 used to describe someone who is highest in rank
I was asked to give my paperwork to the chief clerk.
2 most important, leading
Wheat is the chief crop of the country.
✳ *noun* **chiefs**
a head or leader
The chief of the tribe was a tall, imposing man.

➔ *word family*
chiefly *adverb*
most importantly, mainly

choice /choiss/ *noun* **choices**

1 the act of choosing
He left his job by choice.
2 that which is chosen
I really like your choice of dress.
Italy was her first choice for a holiday.

➔ *collocations*
We **had** a **choice** about where to go on holiday.

We **had no choice but to** go to the police.
It was a **wise choice** to go to the supermarket early
in the morning.

---

choose /chooz/ *verb* **chooses, choosing, chose, chosen**

If you choose something, you select or take what
you prefer.
*Choose something to eat from the restaurant
menu.*

→ *collocations*
*Try and **choose between** the two cars.*
*He **chose to come** home early.*

---

circle /**sir**-kl/

∗ *noun* **circles**
1 a perfectly round shape
My younger brother can draw a perfect circle.
2 a group of people
I have a small circle of very close friends.
∗ *verb* **circles, circling, circled**
1 If you circle something, you move around it.
The dancers were circling the room.
2 If you circle a drawing or piece of writing, you
draw a curved line around it.
I circled the correct word in the puzzle.

---

circumstance /**sir**-cum-stanse/ *noun* **circumstances**
1 a condition connected with an act or event
*We discussed the circumstances surrounding the
robbery with the police.*
2 a state of affairs, often financial
The family are living in very bad circumstances.

→ **collocations**

Under the circumstances, I think his behaviour
was acceptable.
Under no circumstances must you go to the
quarry as it's dangerous there.

---

city /**si**-tee/ noun **cities**

a centre of population larger than a town or village
I live and work in a large city.

---

claim /**clame**/ verb **claims, claiming, claimed**

1 If you claim something, you demand it as a right.
   The man claimed his share of the money.
2 If you claim something, you say it is true.
   She claimed she was born in France.

---

clean /**cleen**/

* adjective **cleaner, cleanest**
1 Something described as clean is free from dirt.
   I need to have very clean hands in order to bake bread.
2 If an official document, such as a driving licence,
   is clean then it means that you have not done
   anything illegal or bad in connection with it.
   I have a clean driving licence because I have never
   been caught speeding.

* adverb
   completely
   The handle of the jug came away clean in my hand.

* verb **cleans, cleaning, cleaned**
   If you clean something, you remove dirt, dust,
   etc, from it.
   I was asked to start cleaning the kitchen.

→ *idioms*

If you **come clean,** you tell the truth about a situation. If you **make a clean breast of something,** you tell the truth about what you have done wrong.

→ *word family*

cleaner /**cleen**-er/ *noun*

someone who is paid to clean

cleanliness /**clen**-lee-ness/ *noun*

the state of being clean

→ *phrases*

Please **clean out** the rabbit hutch.

Why don't you **clean up** that mess?

---

clear /cleer/

* *adjective* **clearer, clearest**

1 easy to hear, see, or understand
   She gave a clear description of the burglar.

2 bright, with no clouds
   The sky was clear.

3 free from difficulties or obstacles
   We are now clear to go on with our plans.

4 obvious
   It was a clear case of mistaken identity.

5 transparent
   The water was clear.

* *verb* **clears, clearing, cleared**

1 If something clears, it is made or becomes clear.
   After the snow storm, the skies cleared.

2 If someone is cleared of something, or their name is cleared, they are proved innocent.
   We spent 10 years trying to clear his name.

3 If you clear an obstacle, you pass through or over it.
   Both horse and rider cleared the fence.

➔ *phrases*
If you clear something away or clear something up, you tidy it up.

➔ *word family*
clearly *adverb*
If you do something clearly, you do it in a way that is clear.

---

clearance /**clee**-ranse/ *noun* **clearances**

1 the act of clearing
She oversaw the clearance of goods from the shelves.

2 permission for something to be done
I received clearance from the boss to take the day off.

---

clever /**cle**-ver/ *adjective* **cleverer, cleverest**

1 able to learn and think quickly
She is a very clever girl and does well at school.

2 able to do things well with the hands, skilful
He is clever at carpentry and makes beautiful furniture.

3 intelligent, ingenious
She found a clever solution to the problem.

➔ *word family*
cleverly *adverb*
If you do something cleverly, you do it in a clever way.
cleverness *noun*
the state of being clever

---

click /**click**/ *noun* **clicks**

a light, sharp sound
He heard the click of her heels on the pavement outside.

client /**clie**-ent/ *noun* **clients**

someone who employs someone else for their service

The lawyer has several clients.

climb /**clime**/

* *verb* **climbs, climbing, climbed**

1 If something climbs, it rises or goes up.
   The plane climbed to its cruising height.
   Stock prices climbed over the weekend.

2 If you climb, you go up using your feet and often your hands.
   Last weekend I climbed a hill.

→ *word family*
   climber *noun*
   someone who climbs

clock /**clok**/ *noun* **clocks**

an instrument that displays the time

close[1] /**cloze**/

* *verb* **closes, closing, closed**

1 If you close something, you shut it.
   Please close the gates when you leave the farm.

2 If you close something, you finish it.
   This final point on the agenda will close the meeting.

* *noun*
   the end
   We will discuss this at close of day.

→ *collocation*
   *We brought the discussion **to a close**.*

close

➔ *phrases*

If something such as a business is **closed down**, it no longer operates.

If you **close in** on something or somebody, you get nearer to it, usually in order to trap it.

If you are **closed in**, you are trapped.

---

close² /close/ *adjective* **closer, closest**

1 near in distance or time, not far
The station is quite close.

2 If you are close to someone, you know and like them well.
We had a nice evening with a few close friends.

3 stuffy or shut in
The air was close in the crowded hall.

➔ *idiom*

If something is **at close quarters,** it is very near to somebody or something else.

---

cloud /clowd/

✳ *noun* **clouds**
a mass of water vapour floating high in the sky
There were large grey clouds in the sky.

✳ *verb* **clouds, clouding, clouded**
If something clouds something else, it darkens it.

➔ *word family*
cloudy /**clow**-dee/ *adjective*
used to describe something that is difficult to see through, or a sky with clouds in it
cloudless /**cloud**-less/ *adjective*
used to describe something that is clear, or a sky without any clouds in it

coach /**coach**/

* *noun* **coaches**
1 a large, comfortable bus
We are taking a coach to the airport.
2 a person who helps a sports team or player improve their skills
The team's new coach has had a great effect on their playing this year.

* *verb* **coaches, coaching, coached**
If you coach a sports person or team, you prepare them for a game or match.
She has been asked to coach the football players on Fridays.

coast /**coast**/

* *noun* **coasts**
the land next to the sea
She lives in a cottage on the coast, overlooking the sea.

* *verb* **coasts, coasting, coasted**
If you coast, you do something without much effort.
I coast along in this job, without doing much.

➔ *idiom*
If **the coast is clear**, you are able to do something without anyone seeing you.

➔ *word family*
coastal /**coe**-stal/ *adjective*
by or near the coast
coastguard /**coast**-gard/ *noun*
the service that rescues boats and swimmers from danger at sea, or a member of that force
An empty boat was spotted by coastguards.

coat /**coat**/

* *noun* **coats**
1   an outer garment with sleeves
    It was snowing so I put my winter coat on.
2   anything that covers something else
    There were three coats of paint on the wall.
* *verb* **coats, coating, coated**
    If you coat something, you cover it.
    The biscuits were coated with chocolate.
→   *word family*
    coating /**coe**-ting/ *noun*
    a covering

code /**co**-de/ *noun* **codes**
1   a collection of laws, rules, or signals
    There is a code of conduct in this office.
2   a method of sending secret messages by using
    signs, sounds, or words
    Try to decipher the message in code.

coffee /**caw**-fee/ *noun* **coffee**
    a dark brown drink brewed from the roasted,
    ground seeds of the coffee tree or shrub
    I drink two cups of coffee every morning.

coin /**coin**/ *noun* **coins**
    a metal piece of money
    I had to put several coins into the parking machine.

cold /**coald**/

* *adjective* **colder, coldest**
1   not hot or warm
    The weather is so cold that I think it might snow.

2 without emotion or excitement, unenthusiastic
His performance in the film left me cold.

3 unfriendly
I felt the other parents gave me a cold welcome.

✳ *noun*

1 absence of heat
I cannot stand the cold.

2 (also **the cold**) an illness, usually consisting of a runny or stuffy nose, sneezing, coughing, aches, and pains
I caught a cold two weeks ago and I still feel unwell.

➔ *usage*
The first noun sense of **cold** is a singular noun.

collapse /cu-**lapse**/

✳ *noun*

1 a fall
A crowd of people witnessed the collapse of the bridge.

2 a failure
We were discussing the possible collapse of the firm because of the economic climate.

✳ *verb* **collapses, collapsing, collapsed**

1 If something collapses, it falls down.
The bridge collapsed after the terrible storm.

2 If you collapse, you lose consciousness.
She collapsed in the extreme heat.

➔ *usage*
The noun **collapse** is singular.

➔ *word family*
collapsible /cu-**lap**-si-bil/ *adjective*
easily made to collapse
The collapsible chair was easily stored away.

college /**col**-edge/ *noun* **colleges**

a place of further education after high school
I went to college when I finished school.

comedy /**com**-ed-ee/ *noun* **comedies**

1 an amusing play, television programme, or film
with a happy ending
I would rather watch a comedy than a drama.

2 the amusing side of something
He had failed to see the comedy of the situation.

➔ *usage*
The second sense of **comedy** has no plural form.

comfort /**cum**-furt/

✴ *noun* **comforts**
1 the state of being free from anxiety, worry, pain,
etc, and having all one's physical needs satisfied
She lives a life of comfort.

2 something that satisfies one's physical needs
We have all modern comforts.

3 strength, hope, sympathy, etc
*They offered comfort to the widow at her husband's
funeral.*

✴ *verb* **comforts, comforting, comforted**
If you comfort someone, you give them strength
and sympathy.
I tried to comfort the widow at her husband's funeral.

➔ *word family*
comfortable /**cumf**-ter-bl/ *adjective*
1 at ease, free from anxiety, worry, etc
I did not feel comfortable in her presence.

2 providing comfort, soft and restful, relaxing

common /**com**-on/ adjective

1   used to describe something that belongs to
     everyone
     *The children played on the common ground behind
     the houses.*

2   used to describe something found everywhere
     It's a common wild flower, but it's still beautiful.

3   used to describe something that or someone who
     is ordinary
     *She felt rather common, sitting with the other girls
     in their beautiful dresses.*

4   used to describe something that happens
     frequently
     His visits have become a common occurrence.

company /**cum**-pa-nee/ noun **companies**

1   a business organization
     She runs a design company.

2   a number of people gathered together by chance
     or invitation
     I asked the company to help themselves.

3   being together with another or others
     I greatly enjoy my friend's company.

compare /com-**pare**/ verb **compares, comparing, compared**

1   If you compare things, you consider them
     together to see how they are alike and different.
     *The police compared the two accounts of the
     accident.*

2   If you compare two things, you point out
     the likenesses and differences between them.
     I compare his novels to those of Dickens.

complain /com-**plane**/ *verb* **complains, complaining, complained**

If you complain about something, you say you are not happy about or satisfied by it.

I complained about the cold weather.

I had to complain to the manager about the faulty goods.

→ *phrase*

If you **complain of something**, you say you are not happy about it.

→ *word family*

complaint /com-**playnt**/ *noun*

a grumble or expression of dissatisfaction

There have been complaints about the service at the hotel.

I had to write a letter of complaint to the manager.

complicate /com-pli-cate/ *verb* **complicates, complicating, complicated**

If you complicate something, you make it difficult.

It will only complicate matters if we travel separately.

→ *word family*

complicated /com-pli-cay-ted/ *adjective*

1 difficult to understand

It's a complicated problem that is difficult to explain.

2 confusing because of having many parts

This is a complicated machine and it takes a while to learn to use it.

computer /com-**pyoo**-ter/ *noun* **computers**

an electronic machine capable of storing and processing large amounts of information and of doing calculations

concert /**con**-sert/ *noun* **concerts**

a musical entertainment
I went to my favourite singer's concert last night.

condition /con-**di**-shun/ *noun* **conditions**

1 the state that someone or something is in
The furniture is in poor condition and must be thrown out.
The patients are in no condition to be sent home.
2 something that must be or happen before something else can take place
A condition of the agreement is that he cannot see his children during the week.

conduct

* *verb* /con-**duct**/ **conducts, conducting, conducted**
If you conduct someone or something, you lead or guide them.
The usher will conduct us to our seats.
* *noun* /**con**-duct/
Your conduct is how you behave.
His conduct on the trip was appalling and he was sent home.

confuse /con-**fyooz**/ *verb* **confuses, confusing, confused**

1   If you confuse something, you put it into disorder, or muddle it.
    I have confused the arrangements by insisting on coming early.

2   If you are confused by something or someone, you are puzzled or bewildered by it or them.
    I was very confused by the questions on the form.

→ *word family*
    confusion /con-**fyoo**-zhun/ *noun*

1   disorder
    a room in total confusion.

2   puzzlement, bewilderment
    There was some confusion over the meaning of the word.

connect /co-**nect**/ *verb* **connects, connecting, connected**

1   If you connect two things, you join them.
    I had to connect the two pipes.

2   If you connect a thing or idea with another one, you relate them to one another.
    He didn't connect the middle-aged woman with the girl he used to know.
    The police are connecting the two murders.

→ *idiom*
    If you are **well connected,** you are related to important or powerful people.

→ *word family*
    connection /co-**nec**-shun/ *noun*

1   something that joins things
    There is a loose connection between the two pipes.

2 something that makes one think of a certain person, place, event, etc, when one sees another
Police are making a connection between the crimes.

---

constant /**con**-stant/ *adjective*

1 used to describe something that never stops
The noise of the rain is constant.

2 used to describe something that does not change
Try to keep the temperature of the room at a constant level.

➜ *word family*
constantly /**con**-stant-lee/ *adverb*

1 again and again, nearly always, regularly
The children are constantly nagging for attention.

2 without stopping
The lights of the house have been burning constantly.

---

consult /con-**sult**/ *verb* **consults, consulting, consulted**

1 If you consult someone about something, you ask them for advice, information, or help.
I need to consult a doctor about my headaches.

2 If you consult with someone, you discuss matters with them.
He had to consult his partners about the proposed business deal.

3 If you consult something about another thing, you look it up.
I must consult a dictionary.

➜ *word family*
consultation /con-sul-**tay**-shun/ *noun*
a meeting with someone to ask for advice or information

consumer /con-**syoo**-mer/ *noun* **consumers**

a person who buys or uses goods

You can return faulty goods to the shop as you have consumers' rights.

contain /con-**tane**/ *verb* **contains, containing, contained**

1   If something contains something else, it has it in it.
     The bucket contains a gallon of water.
2   If you contain something, you keep control of it.
     We cannot contain the fire.

→   *usage*
     Remember, don't use **containing** for **contain**, so the bucket **contained** water not **was containing** water.

→   *word family*
     container /con-**tay**-ner/ *noun*
     anything made to hold something else in it
     a plant container

contemporary /con-**tem**-po-ra-ree/

*   *adjective*
1   belonging to the same time
     We read a contemporary record of the war.
2   used to describe something that is modern
     I really like watching contemporary dance.

*   *noun* **contemporaries**
     someone who lives or lived at the same time as another person
     The man was a contemporary of my grandfather.

content¹ /**con**-tent/ *noun* **contents**

something which is in something else
The content of his lunchbox was unappealing.

content² /con-**tent**/ *adjective*

satisfied, pleased, not wanting more than one
has

His parents were content with his exam results.

➔ **word family**

contentment /con-**tent**-ment/ *noun*

the state of feeling satisfied or pleased

contrast

✳ *verb* /con-**trast**/ **contrasts, contrasting,
contrasted**

1 If you contrast two things, you put them
together to show the differences between
them.

*Contrast their nice, neat garden with our sloppy
one.*

2 If something contrasts with something else, it
appears very different to it.

*The black dress contrasts beautifully with her
blonde hair.*

✳ *noun* /**con**-trast/ **contrasts**

a clear difference

There is a stark contrast between the two brothers.

control /con-**trole**/

✳ *noun* **controls**

1 power over the movements and actions of
another person or thing

The country is under the control of a tyrant.

2 power over one's own thoughts and feelings

*We were amazed she could keep her temper under
control.*

3   (controls) the parts of a machine that start, stop, or change the movement of all the other parts
She studied the controls of the plane.

✳   verb **controls, controlling, controlled**

1   If you control something, you have power or authority over it.
My sister controls the whole department.

2   If you control a machine, you direct its movements.
She controls the car well at high speeds.

3   If you control yourself, you hold back or restrain yourself.
I was so angry that I could no longer control myself.

➔   *word family*
controller /con-**troe**-ler/ *noun*
someone who controls something, especially a machine

conversation /con-ver-**say**-shun/ *noun* **conversations**

talk, speech with others
We had a long conversation about the weather.

cool /**cool**/

✳   *adjective* **cooler, coolest**

1   slightly cold, pleasantly cold
It's pleasant to have a cool drink on a hot day.

2   calm, not easily excited
Always try and keep cool in difficult situations.

✳   *verb* **cools, cooling, cooled**

1   If you cool something, you make it colder.
Cool the soup before freezing it.

2 If you cool down, you become less hot or calmer or less interested.

She was very angry at first but she cooled down later.

➔ **word family**

coolness *noun*

the state of being cool

---

cope /**cope**/ *verb* **copes, coping, coped**

If you cope with something, you deal with it successfully.

He's finding it difficult to cope with his workload.

---

copy /**cop**-ee/

* *noun* **copies**

1 a thing done or made in exactly the same way as another

Can I get a copy of the photo?

2 a single example of a newspaper, magazine, book, etc

I ordered several copies of the book.

* *verb* **copies, copying, copied**

If you copy something, you make a copy of it.

---

core /**core**/

* *noun* **cores**

1 the central part of a fruit in which the seeds are stored

I discarded the apple core.

2 the innermost part, the most important part

We must get to the core of the problem.

* *verb* **cores, coring, cored**

remove the core from something

I cored the apple with a special tool.

corner /**cawr**-ner/

∗ *noun* **corners**

1   the meeting place of two walls
    We're sitting at a table in the corner of the room.

2   a difficult position
    He is in a tight corner financially.

∗ *verb* **corners, cornering, cornered**
    If you are cornered, you are put into a difficult situation
    The journalist cornered the politician by asking awkward questions.

➔ *phrase*
    If something is **around the corner,** it is about to happen soon.

correct /co-**rect**/

∗ *adjective*
    right, having no mistakes
    Could you tell me the correct spelling of your name?

∗ *verb* **corrects, correcting, corrected**

1   If you correct someone, you tell them what is wrong with their knowledge or opinions.
    He corrected her belief that he was from France.

2   If you correct something, you point out mistakes.
    She corrected the student's homework.

➔ *word family*
    correctness /co-**rect**-ness/ *noun*
    the state of being correct
    correction /co-**rect**-shun/ *noun*

1   the act of correcting

2   the right thing put in place of a mistake
    She had to write all her corrections in red.

cost /cost/

* *verb* **costs, costing, cost**

1 If something costs a certain price, it is on sale for that price.
The cards cost a pound each.

2 If something costs something else, it causes loss or suffering.
The battle cost many lives.

* *noun* **costs**

1 the price
We could just afford the cost of the house.

2 loss
The war was won, but at the cost of many lives.

cough /cof/

* *verb* **coughs, coughing, coughed**
If you cough, you force air noisily from the throat, to clear it of some matter such as dust or phlegm.
I coughed loudly.

* *noun* **coughs**

1 a noisy forcing of the air from the throat
He had a nasty sounding cough.

2 an illness marked by frequent coughing
I have had a bad cough for weeks.

council /coun-sil/ *noun* **councils**

a group of people chosen to make decisions, to advise, or to discuss issues affecting a larger number of people
The city council is in charge of the library service.

➔ *word family*
councillor /**coun**-si-lor/ *noun*
a member of a council

➔ *usage*
Remember not to confuse **council** with **counsel,**
meaning to give someone advice.

---

counter /**coun**-ter/

✳ *noun* **counters**
1   a person or thing that counts
They work as counters of votes at elections.
2   the table in a shop, across which goods are sold
I took my book to the shop counter.
✳ *verb* **counters, countering, countered**
If you counter something, you act in order to
oppose it or defend yourself against it.
*The battalion countered the enemy attack by
bringing in more soldiers.*

---

courage /**cur**-age/ *noun*

bravery
He showed great courage in the face of danger.

---

course /**coarse**/ *noun* **courses**
1   the way along which a thing moves or runs
*We paddled our canoes along the course of the
river.*
2   a number of lectures or lessons given for the
same purpose
I would like to take a business course.
3   a part of a meal served at one time
The meal consisted of three courses.

court /**coart**/ *noun* **courts**

1 a place marked out for sports
My brother and I went to the tennis court for a game.

2 the building in which judges hear cases and give decisions
The lawyer had to go to court to defend her client.

cover /**cu**-ver/ *verb* **covers, covering, covered**

1 If you cover something, you put something else over it.
I covered the table with a cloth.

2 If something covers something else, it includes it.
The cost covers the room and all meals.

→ *word family*
covering /**cuv**-ring/ *noun*
anything that covers something
The was a light covering of snow on the grass.

crash /**crash**/

* *verb* **crashes, crashing, crashed**

1 If something crashes, it falls with a loud noise.
The plate crashed to the floor.

2 If one thing crashes against another, it dashes violently against it.
He crashed his fist into the wall.

* *noun* **crashes**

1 a breakage or wreckage
There was a terrible car crash on the road today.

2 the sudden failure of a business or market
We remembered the crash of his firm.

crazy /**cray**-zee/ *adjective*

used to say that someone or something is mad or stupid

He must be crazy to think that.

→ *collocation*

*My mum will **go crazy** when she sees this mess.*

→ *phrase*

If you're **crazy about** someone or something, you like them or it very much.

creature /**cree**-chur/ *noun* **creatures**

anything living that is not a plant, especially humans or animals

There are wild creatures that only come out at night.

credit /**cre**-dit/

* *noun*

1 a system of buying goods or services and paying for them later

I bought the car on credit.

2 approval or praise

The police gave him credit for capturing the thief.

→ *collocation*

*I got **the credit** for the idea, even though it wasn't mine.*

*My brother will **take the credit** for doing the chores.*

* *verb* **credits, crediting, credited**

1 If you credit a bank account, you put money into it.

I credited my account with the money my mother gave me.

2 If you credit something, you believe it.

I could not credit how late he was.

→ *phrases*

If you **credit someone with something,** you say they are responsible for something good or well done. If you **credit something to someone,** you say they are responsible for it.

---

crime /**crime**/ *noun*

illegal activity

→ *collocation*

He committed **the crime of** murder.

→ *usage*

Remember that someone **commits a crime** rather than **makes** or **does a crime.**

→ *word family*

criminal /**cri**-mi-nal/ *adjective*

1   used to describe something that is against the law

He was convicted of a criminal act.

2   used to describe something that is wrong or wicked

It was utterly criminal to cut down such a beautiful tree.

✳   *noun* **criminals**

someone who breaks the law

---

crisis /**crie**-sis/ *noun* **crises** /**crie**-seez/

1   a turning point at which things must become either better or worse

Her illness came to a crisis suddenly during the night.

2   a very serious state of affairs

The firm recovered from a financial crisis.

criticize /cri-ti-size/ verb criticizes, criticizing, criticized

1   If you criticize something, you point out the good and bad in it.
    I criticized his writing constructively.
2   If you criticize something, you find fault with it.
    His mother was always criticizing his clothes.

crop /crop/

*   noun **crops**
    all the grain, fruit, etc, that is grown or gathered at one place or time
    The wheat crop was ruined by the wet weather.
*   verb **crops, cropping, cropped**
    If you crop something, you cut it short.
    She cropped her hair short.
➜   **phrases**
    If something or someone **crops up**, they turn up unexpectedly.
    *Difficulties **cropped up**.*
    If something or someone **comes a cropper**, they fall heavily or fail completely at something.
    *He **came a cropper** on the icy surface.*

crucial /croo-shal/ adjective

    of the greatest importance, needing a clear decision
    He decided to take the crucial step of resigning from his job.

crush /crush/

*   verb **crushes, crushing, crushed**
    If you crush something, you squeeze it with force.
    I crushed the banana with a fork.

* *noun* **crushes**
1 the crowding together of things or people
People were hurt in the crush.
2 an attraction
She has a crush on the new boy.
→ *word family*
crushing /cru-shing/ *adjective*
embarrassing, inflicting great damage
The game's outcome was a crushing defeat for the home team.

cry /crie/

* *verb* **cries, crying, cried**
1 If you cry, you weep.
I cried when I left home.
2 If you cry, you shout loudly.
They were stuck in the lift, so they cried for help.
* *noun* **cries**
a loud shout
His cry was not heard through the thick walls.

culture /cul-chur/ *noun* cultures

1 the character of an age and people as seen through their customs, arts, etc
I would like to learn about Roman culture.
2 learning and good taste
They describe themselves as people of culture because they attend the opera.
→ *word family*
cultural *adjective*
used to describe something relating to culture
It is a book on cultural changes in the country.

current /**cur**-ent/

✳ *adjective*
belonging to the present time
These trousers are in the current fashion.

✳ *noun* **currents**
1 a stream of water or air moving in a certain direction
The current of the river is very strong.
2 a flow of electricity
The electrical current was cut and the lights went out.

damage /**da**-midge/

✳ *noun* **damages**
1 injury, harm
The recent storm caused a lot of damage.
2 (**damages** /**da**–mi-jeez/) money paid to make up for loss or harm
She sued the driver of the car that hit her for damages.

✳ *verb* **damages, damaging, damaged**
If you damage something, you harm it.
I damaged the door when I slammed it shut.

➜ *usage*
Damage is **caused** or **done**, but never made.

dark /**dark**/

✳ *adjective* **darker, darkest**
1 without light
The nights are dark.
2 having black or brown hair
She met a tall dark stranger.

✳ *noun* /**dark**/
the absence of light, also called **darkness**.
He was not visible in the dark.

➜ *word family*
darken /**dar**-ken/ *verb*
to make or become darker
Her fair skin had been darkened by the sun.

daughter /**daw**-ter/ *noun* **daughters**

a parent's female child
I have two daughters and a son.

day /**day**/ *noun* **days**

1 one of the seven, 24-hour periods in a week
There are 365 days in a year.
2 the time during a 24-hour period when it is light
I can only go out during the day, not at night.
➜ ***word family***
daylight *noun*
light given off by the sun, rather than other light
sources
I could see daylight through the crack in the door.

daydream /**day**-dreem/ *verb* **daydreams, daydreaming,**
daydreamed

to dream while not asleep
I daydream of being rich one day.

dead /**ded**/

✱ *adjective*
1 no longer living
My brother has been dead for ten years.
2 dull, lifeless
She wore a dead expression on her face.
3 absolute, complete
The car came to a dead stop.
4 not working
The phone is dead.
✱ *adverb*
1 completely
I'm dead tired after working all weekend.

2 straight

The house is dead ahead.

→ *usage*

If you are talking about dead people collectively, you can say **the dead**.

→ *word family*

deaden /**de**-den/ *verb*

If something is deadened, it is dulled or lessened.

This pill should deaden the pain.

deadly /**ded**-lee/ *adjective*

capable of causing death

He was guilty of assault with a deadly weapon.

deal /deel/

✳ *noun* **deals**

1 a business agreement

We are about to sign an important export deal.

2 an amount

He earns a great deal of money.

✳ *verb* **deals, dealing, dealt** /**delt**/

1 If you deal with someone, you do business with them.

I will only deal with the owner of the firm.

2 If you deal with something, you cope with or handle it.

I cannot deal with this problem just now.

3 If you deal cards, you give them out.

Can you deal the cards please?

→ *word family*

dealer /**dee**-ler/ *noun*

1 a person who buys and sells objects

She is a successful dealer in antiques.

2 a person who gives out playing cards in a game
Who's the dealer in this card game?

dear /deer/

* *adjective* **dearer, dearest**
1 well loved
I received a letter from my dear mother.
2 expensive, high in price
The oranges are dear today.
* *noun* **dears**
    a loved person
    He is such a dear.
→ ***word family***
    dearly /**deer**-leè/ ad*verb*
    If you love or care for someone dearly, you do so
    very much.

death /deth/ *noun* **deaths**

1 the act of dying
Today is the second anniversary of my father's death.
2 the state of being dead
Drinking poison can lead to death.
→ ***collocation***
    *If he goes out to sea in this storm, he faces **certain death**.*
→ ***word family***
    deathly /**deth**-lee/ *adjective, adverb*
    like death
    Her face is deathly pale.

debt /det/ *noun* **debts**

anything owed
He has run up a lot of debt over the years.

deep /**deep**/ adjective **deeper, deepest**

1 used to describe something that goes far down
He fell in a deep hole.

2 serious or strongly felt
He has very deep feelings for her.

3 cunning
The film has a deep plot.

4 If a sound is deep, it is low in pitch.
A deep, resonant sound came from the tuba.

5 If a colour is deep, it is strong or dark.
She wore a deep purple coat.

→ *idiom*
You can use **the deep** to mean the sea.

→ *word family*
deepen /**dee**-pen/ verb
If something deepens, it becomes deeper.
His voice deepened when he started to sing.

degree /di-**gree**/ noun **degrees**

1 a step or stage
They are making progress by degrees.

2 a unit of measurement for heat, angles, etc
Preheat the oven to 180 degrees.

3 the award given by a university to those who reach a certain standard of learning
I have a degree in mathematics.

→ *phrase*
If something is true **to a degree,** it is true partially, or to an extent.

delicate /**de**-li-kit/ adjective

1 fine, easily hurt, or damaged
The vase is made of very delicate porcelain.

2 fine, dainty
She has particularly delicate features.
3 not very healthy, easily made ill
My son has a very delicate constitution.
4 light, subtle
The walls were painted a delicate shade of pink.
➔ **word family**
delicacy /**de**-li-ca-see/ *noun*
1 a fine, high quality and delicious food
Amongst the delicacies on offer was caviar.
2 the state of being impressively fine or elegant
The delicacy of the embroidery was inspiring.

design /di-**zine**/
* ✳ *verb* **designs, designing, designed**
If you design something, you make a plan for it to be made or developed.
He designed a swimming pool for the community centre.
* ✳ *noun* **designs**
1 a plan or drawing of something to be made
We are looking forward to seeing the design for the new building.
2 a plan, a purpose
They met by design.

desire /di-**zire**/
* ✳ *verb* **desires, desiring, desired**
1 If you desire something, you wish or long for it.
I only desire to be happy.
2 If you desire someone, you are physically attracted to them.
She desired the man in the sandwich shop.

detail

* *noun* **desires**
1 a longing, a wish
   She expressed a desire to emigrate.
2 a strong physical attraction to someone
   Her desire for him was obvious.
3 something or someone that is desired
   This house is his heart's desire.

detail /**dee**-tale, di-**tale**/
* *verb* **details, detailing, detailed**
   If you detail something, you give a very full account or description of it.
   I started detailing the tasks to be carried out.
* *noun* **details**
   a small part or item
   Please tell me all the details of the conversation.
→ *word family*
   detailed /**dee**-taild, di-**taild**/ *adjective*
   very full and exact
   She asked for a detailed report.

develop /di-**ve**-lop/ *verb* **develops, developing, developed**
1 If something develops, it grows bigger or better.
   The plan is slowly developing.
2 If you develop something, you make it grow bigger or better.
   You must exercise to develop your muscles.
→ *word family*
   development /di-**ve**-lop-ment/ *noun*
1 growth
   I am very interested in early childhood development.
   It was good to see the development of the business.

2 a stage of growth
Please let us know of the latest developments.
3 a new product or invention
There are exciting new developments in industry.

dig /**dig**/ *verb* **digs, digging, dug**
1 If you dig earth or soil, you turn it up with a spade.
I spent the day digging in the garden.
2 If you dig someone, you prod or poke them.
I tried to dig her in the ribs to stop her talking.
3 If you dig in or for something, you search in or for it.
She dug in her purse for her house keys.
➔ *word family*
digger /**di**-ger/ *noun*
a machine that digs earth or soil

direction /di-**rec**-shun/ *noun* **directions**
1 the way in which someone or something is looking, pointing, going, etc
The house faces a northerly direction.
➔ *collocation*
*Could you point me in **the direction of** the shops?*
2 (**directions**) instructions for getting somewhere or doing something
Can you give me directions to the station?
➔ *collocation*
*I find it difficult to **follow directions**.*

dirty /**dur**-tee/ *adjective* **dirtier, dirtiest**
1 unclean
My hands are very dirty.
2 mean or unfair
He played a really dirty trick on us.

discovery /dis-**cu**-ve-ree/ *noun* **discoveries**

1   the act of finding
    They went on a voyage of discovery.

2   something that has been found out
    They made a number of important discoveries.

discuss /di-**scus**/ *verb* **discusses, discussing, discussed**

If you discuss something, you talk about it.
We were discussing the possibility of going to the cinema.

→ *word family*

discussion /di-**scu**-shun/ *noun*
the act of talking about something

→ *usage*

Remember that you always **discuss something**, you don't just **discuss**.

distance /dis-tanse/ *noun* **distances**

1   being far off
    I live at quite a distance from my mother.

2   the space between two points or places
    There is a distance of three miles between the villages.

3   unfriendliness
    I noticed a certain distance in his manner.

→ *word family*

distant /**dis**-tant/ *adjective*

1   used to describe something that is far off
    I like to travel to distant lands.

2   used to describe something, such as a relationship, that is not close
    I met a distant relative completely by accident.

3 used to describe a cold or unfriendly manner
He seemed rather distant to his old friends.

distribute /dis-**tri**-byoot, dis-tri-**byoot**/ *verb* **distributes, distributing, distributed**

1 If you distribute something, you give each person his or her share.
The charity has been distributing food to the poor.

2 If something is distributed, it is spread out widely.
There are fast food restaurants distributed throughout the country.

➜ *word family*
distribution /dis-tri-**byoo**-shun/ *noun*
the act of giving things out to people

division /di-**vi**-zhun/ *noun* **divisions**

1 the act of dividing
He was worried about the division of responsibility within the department.

2 one of the parts into which something is divided
He works in the sales division of the firm.

3 disagreement
There has been a great division in the family.

do /doo/ *verb* **does, doing, did** /did/, **done** /dun/

1 You use do with another verb to ask questions and make negative statements.
Do you like chocolate?
I do not want to go to the park.

2 If you do something, you perform an action.
I was doing the dishes.

3 If you do something, you make or perform it.
I'm doing spaghetti for supper.

➔ *phrases*

If you **do something badly,** you do not do it well.

If you **do something well,** you perform it well.

If you have **something to do with something,** you are connected to it in some way.

If you **do away with something,** you get rid of it.

If you **do without something,** you don't have it.

➔ *usage*

The negative form of do is **do not** or **don't.**

---

dog /**dawg**/

* *noun* **dogs**
a common domestic animal with fur and four legs
I have a very hairy dog.

* *verb* **dogs, dogging** /**daw**-ging/, **dogged** /**dawgd**/
If you dog someone, you follow them closely.
He was dogged by the journalists all the way home.

➔ *word family*
dogged /**daw**-ged/ *adjective*
single-minded, determined
He showed dogged determination in getting the job.

---

door /**dore**/ *noun* **doors**

a moveable barrier in an entrance to a building or room
Could you close the door when you leave the room?

---

doubt /**dout**/

* *verb* **doubts, doubting, doubted**
If you doubt something, you are uncertain about it.
I doubt whether they'll come at this time of night.

✳ *noun* **doubts**
a feeling of uncertainty
I have doubts about his suitability for the job.

➜ *word family*
doubtful /dout-ful/ *adjective*
used to describe something that probably is not
true

drain /drane/

✳ *verb* **drains, draining, drained**
1 If you drain liquid, you draw it off using pipes
and ditches.
The plumber drained the water tank.
2 If you drain something, you empty it completely.
He quickly drained his glass.
✳ *noun* **drains**
a pipe or channel to carry away liquid
The drains under the house are blocked.

draw /draw/

✳ *verb* **draws, drawing, drew** /droo/, **drawn** /dron/
1 If you draw a picture, you make it with a pencil,
pen, or crayons.
I asked my brother to draw a picture of our house.
2 If you draw attention, you attract it.
*I tried to draw his attention to the lack of money in
our bank account.*
3 If you draw towards something, you move near to it.
The crowd drew nearer as the boats approached.
4 If two teams or opponents draw in a game, it
ends with nobody winning.
The teams drew 1–1.

✱ *noun* **draws**
1 an attraction
   The new singer is a real draw at the club.
2 a game or contest won by nobody
   The football match ended in a draw.
➜ *phrases*
   If you **draw the line at** something, you refuse to do it.
   If something **draws up** somewhere, it stops there.
   If you **draw up** something, you prepare it, especially in writing.

dream /dreem/

✱ *noun* **dreams**
1 the ideas or fancies passing through the mind of a person sleeping
   I had a very frightening dream last night.
2 memories of the past or thoughts of what may happen
   I have a dream of becoming a millionaire.
✱ *verb* **dreams, dreaming, dreamt /dremt/ or dreamed /dreemd/**
1 If you dream, you have ideas or fancies passing through your mind when you are asleep.
   I dreamt about my childhood home last night.
2 If you dream about something, you imagine it.
   I dream of emigrating to a hot country.

dress /dress/

✱ *verb* **dresses, dressing, dressed**
1 If you dress, you put on clothes.
   I dressed warmly as it was cold outside.

2 If you dress, you wear a certain style of clothes, for example, formal or evening.
Do we have to dress for dinner?

＊ *noun* **dresses**

1 a piece of clothing worn by women, with a skirt and top joined together
I was wearing a summer dress.

2 clothing in general
I wore casual dress to the party.

➔ *phrases*
If you **dress up,** you put on the clothing of another person, nation, etc.
If you **dress up for** something, you put on your best clothing for an event.

➔ *usage*
Remember that you **get dressed**, you don't **dressed**.

➔ *collocation*
If you put on **fancy dress,** you wear a costume.

---

drink /dringk/

＊ *verb* **drinks, drinking**, **drank /drangk/**, **drunk /drungk/**

1 If you drink, you swallow a liquid.
I sat and drank my cup of tea.

2 If you drink, you take alcoholic liquor.
Her husband drinks an awful lot.

＊ *noun* **drinks**

1 an act of drinking
If you're thirsty, have a drink of water.

2 a liquid suitable for drinking
Would you like a drink?

3 alcoholic liquor
It's best to avoid drink if you are unwell.

4 a glass of alcoholic liquor
I'll have one drink and then I must leave.

➜ *phrase*
If you **drink to** something, you celebrate
someone's health or happiness with a drink.

drive /drive/

✳ *verb* **drives, driving**, **drove** /drove/, **driven** /dri-ven/

1 If you drive, you control or guide a car.
I dream of driving a sports car.

2 If you drive something or someone along, you
force or urge them.
The farmer drove his cows to market.

4 If you drive something into something else, you
hit it hard.
I tried to drive the nail through the wood.

✳ *noun* **drives**

1 a ride in a car
We are going for a drive in the countryside.

2 a private road up to a house
The drive was a mile long.

3 energy
She has a lot of energy and drive.

➜ *phrase*
If you **drive someone mad**, you annoy them.

drop /drop/

✳ *noun* **drops**

1 a very small amount of liquid
I did not spill a drop of milk.

2 the act of falling
There has been a real drop in temperature this week.

3   the distance that a person may fall
He fell a drop of 300 feet from the castle wall.

*   *verb* **drops, dropping, dropped** /dropt/

1   If you drop, you fall
I dropped down from the wall.

2   If you drop something, you let it fall.
I dropped a plate on the floor.

3   If an amount of something drops, it falls or is caused to fall to a lower level or amount
The price dropped sharply.
The driver was forced to drop his speed quickly.

---

dry /drie/

*   *adjective* **drier, driest**

1   not wet or damp
The paint is not yet dry.

2   with little rainfall
We have just had an unusually dry spell.

*   *verb* **dries, drying, dried**
If you dry something, you make it not wet.
I was drying my hair when the phone rang.

➜   *phrases*
If you **dry something off,** you make it dry.
If something **dries up,** there is nothing more of it.

---

dust /dust/

*   *noun*
tiny dry particles of earth or matter
The house is full of dust.

*   *verb* **dusts, dusting, dusted**

1   If you dust, you use a cloth to remove tiny dry particles that lie on objects.
I must dust the piano.

2 If you dust with something, you sprinkle powder over something else.

I dusted the cake with icing sugar.

→ **word family**

dusty /**dus**-tee/ *adjective*

used to describe something that is covered in dust

dustbin /**dust**-bin/ *noun* **dustbins**

a container for rubbish or waste

each /**eech**/ *pronoun, adjective*

every one taken singly or separately

Each pupil is to bring money for the school trip.

→ **usage**

Each is always used before a singular noun, as in **each person**, not **each people**.

ear /**eer**/ *noun* **ears**

1 the organ of hearing

She has a very sore ear.

2 the ability to hear the difference between sounds

He has a very musical ear.

3 someone's attention

The senator is known to have the president's ear.

early /**ur**-lee/

* *adjective* **earlier, earliest**

1 before the time arranged

We were surprised by her sister's early arrival.

2 near the beginning

It happened during the early part of the century.

3 belonging to the first stages of development, etc
He is an expert in early musical instruments.

✶ *adverb*

1 near the beginning of a period of time
They were meeting early in the afternoon.

2 sooner than usual, sooner than expected, sooner than necessary, or sooner than often
I try to arrive early for work.

---

earth /**urth**/ *noun*

1 (often **Earth**) the planet on which we live
People used to think that the Earth was flat.

2 the ground or soil
I was digging the earth to plant some trees.

3 the world as opposed to heaven
He would move heaven and earth to be with his family during this difficult time.

---

eat /**eet**/ *verb* **eats, eating, ate** /**ate**/**, eaten** /**ee**-ten/

If you eat, you chew and swallow food.
My sister eats a lot of chocolate.
I eat only vegetarian food.

---

edge /**edge**/

✶ *noun* **edges**

1 the sharp side of a blade
The knife had a very sharp edge.

2 a border or boundary
I was sitting at the edge of the lake.

✶ *verb* **edges, edging, edged**

If you edge towards something, you move there gradually, especially with small sideways movements.
He edged his way towards the front of the line.

educate /e-ju-cate/ *verb* **educates, educating, educated**

If you educate someone, you teach or train them.
The school educates children to the age of eighteen.

→ *word family*

education /e-ju-**cay**-shun/ *noun*
the act of educating
She wanted her children to get a good education.
educational /e-ju-**cay**-shu-nal/ *adjective*
connected with education
She only buys educational toys.

effect /i-**fect**/

* *noun* **effects**

1 a result
The medicine had little effect.
The angry words had no effect on the child's behaviour.

2 an impression
The flower arrangements created a colourful effect.

3 (**effects**) lighting and sounds used in a play, television programme, or film
I was so impressed by the effects in the stage show.

→ *collocation*
*The film's **special effects** were very realistic.*

* *verb* **effects, effecting, effected**
If you effect something, you bring it about.
The company's actions were effecting a market change.

→ *usage*
Remember not to confuse the word **effect**, with the verb **affect**.

egg /**eg**/ *noun* **eggs**

1   an object, usually covered with a hard brittle shell, laid by a bird or reptile, from which a young one is hatched
The chicken was sitting on the eggs that she's laid.

2   such an object laid by the domestic hen and used as food
I always have a boiled egg for breakfast.

elastic /ee-**la**-stic/ *adjective*

used to describe something that is able to stretch or be stretched easily, but returning immediately to its former shape
My grandmother wears a skirt with an elastic waistband.

elect /i-**lect**/

*   *verb* **elects, electing, elected**

1   If you elect to do something, you choose to do it.
I always elect to travel by train.

2   If you elect a person or party, you choose them by voting.
We voted to elect a new president.

*   *adjective*
having been chosen but not yet doing the job
He is the president elect.

➜   *word family*
election /i-**lec**-shun/ *noun*
the act of choosing, especially by a vote
We can look forward to an exciting presidential election.

electric /i-**lec**-tric/

* *adjective*

1 having to do with electricity
   I have an electric toothbrush.

2 exciting, thrilling
   The singer gave an electric performance.

* *noun* **electrics**

   (electrics) electric fittings
   We need to replace the electrics in the house.

else /**elss**/ *adjective*

1 besides, also
   What else did he say?
   Who else spoke?

2 other than that already mentioned
   I love London, but have decided to live somewhere else.

→ *idiom*

   If you tell someone to do something **or else**, you
   are saying (usually as a joke) that they must do it.

emergency /i-**mer**-jen-see/ *noun* **emergencies**

   a state of affairs requiring immediate action
   Call the police in an emergency.

emotion /i-**mo**-shun/ *noun* **emotions**

1 strong or deep feeling
   He felt strong emotions towards his friends.

2 the moving or upsetting of the mind or feelings
   I was overcome by emotion watching the sad film.

→ *word family*

   emotional /i-**moe**-she-nal/ *adjective*

1 of the emotions
   The child has emotional problems.

2 causing or showing deep feelings
an emotional farewell
3 easily moved by emotion
a very emotional person

employ /im-**ploy**/ *verb* **employs, employing, employed**

1 If you employ someone, you give work to them.
The firm employs hundreds of factory workers.
2 If you employ something, you use it.
He employed tact when speaking to his boss.

➔ *word family*

employee /im-**ploy**-ee/ *noun*
a person paid to work for another person or for a firm
The firm had to sack several of its employees.
employer /im-**ploy**-er/ *noun*
someone who gives work to another person
employment /im-**ploy**-ment/ *noun*
job, occupation
Employment is not easy to find at the moment.

end /**end**/

* *noun* **ends**
1 the last part of anything
I have reached the end of the book.
2 another word for death
The gangster met a violent end.
3 a purpose or aim
Let's work towards such an end.
* *verb* **ends, ending, ended**
If you end something, you make it stop or finish.
The two countries have agreed to end the fighting.

energy /e-ner-jee/ noun energies

active power, force, vigour

She lacks energy since her illness.

engage /en-**gage**/ verb engages, engaging, engaged

1 If you engage someone, you give them work.
   We have engaged a gardener to work on the grounds.

2 If military forces engage with one another, they begin fighting.
   engage in warfare

3 If you engage yourself with something, you make yourself busy.
   I engaged myself with housework for most the day.

4 If you engage someone's attention, you attract it.
   I tried to engage the child's attention.

➔ **word family**

engaged /en-**gaged**/ adjective

When a couple are engaged, they are going to get married.

engine /**in**-jin/ noun engines

a machine that produces power

The car engine made a very strange noise.

enough /i-**nuf**/

✳ adjective

as many or as much as is required

Can you make enough food for the four of them?

✳ noun

a sufficient amount

I have eaten enough to last me a week.

She does not eat enough fruit and vegetables.

enter /**en**-ter/ *verb* **enters, entering, entered**

1 If you enter somewhere, you go or come into it.
I entered the building by the back door.

2 If you enter a job or activity, you start to do it.
I thought about entering politics.

3 If you enter something in writing, you write or type it.
I entered the plumber's contact details into my phone.

➔ *word family*
entrant /**en**-trant/ *noun* **entrants**
someone who enters something
There were 400 entrants in the race.

entry /**en**-tree/ *noun* **entries**

1 the act of entering
I tried to gain entry to the locked building.

2 a way in
This door is the only entry to the block of flats.

3 something written in a diary, book, blog, etc
I read out the blog entry she wrote yesterday.

➔ *word family*
entrance /**en**-transe/ *noun* **entrances**
a point of entry
Where is the entrance to the museum?

equal /**ee**-kwal/

✳ *adjective*

1 the same in size, number, value, etc
My husband and I have equal salaries.

2 able to do something
I feel he is not equal to the task.

✳ *noun* **equals**
a person the same as another in rank or ability
They are a good match: he's her intellectual equal.

* *verb* **equals**, **equalling**, **equalled**

If something equals something else, it is the same as it.

This year's sales figures equal last year's figures.

➔ *word family*

equality /i-**kwol**-i-tee/ *noun*

the state of being treated the same as other people

the fight for racial equality

equalize /**ee**-kwol-ize/ *verb*

to make or become equal (for example, a score)

The home team equalized just before the end.

error /**e**-ror/ *noun* **errors**

1 a mistake

He made several spelling errors in his report.

2 the state of being mistaken

The letter was sent to your address in error.

establish /i-**sta**-blish/ *verb* **establishes**, **establishing**, **established**

1 If you establish something, you set it up.

We are hoping to establish a local branch of the society.

2 If you establish an object, you place or fix it into a position, usually permanently.

They trees were well established in the garden.

➔ *word family*

establishment /es-**tab**-lish-ment/ *noun*

1 the state of being established

2 a business or institution

event /i-**vent**/ *noun* **events**

1 anything that happens, an incident

There were various events leading up to the war.

2 a single race or contest at sports or races
Have you signed up for the athletic events?

---

ever /**e**-ver/ *adverb*

at any time
Have you ever eaten sushi?

---

every /**ev**-ree/ *adjective*

each one
Every child in the class was present.

➔ *usage*
Every is always used before a singular noun, so **every person**, not **every people**.

---

everyone /**ev**-ree-wun/ *pronoun*

every person
Everyone in the room suddenly burst out singing.

---

everything /**ev**-ree-thing/ *pronoun*

all things being considered as a group
Everything in this room is filthy.

---

example /ig-**zam**-pl/ *noun* **examples**

1 one thing chosen to show what others of the same kind are like, a model
This is a wonderful example of the artist's work.
2 a person or thing that deserves to be imitated
The teacher's patience is an example to us all.

---

exchange /iks-**change**/

✱ *verb* **exchanges, exchanging, exchanged**
If you exchange something for another, you give one thing and receive another in its place.
He hopes to exchange his dollars for euros.

* *noun* **exchanges**
the act of exchanging
There was an exchange of views.
My granny gives her neighbours food in exchange
for gardening work.

excuse

* *verb* /ek-**scyooz**/ **excuses, excusing, excused**
1 If you excuse someone, you let them off from
doing something.
I am excused from playing football because of my
twisted ankle.
2 If you excuse someone, you forgive them.
She asked to be excused for her late arrival.

* *noun* /ek-**scyooss**/ **excuses**
a reason given for failure or wrongdoing
I gave an excuse for not going to my class.

→ *word family*
excusable /ek-**scyoo**-za-bl/ *adjective*
used to describe something that can be forgiven

exercise /ek-**ek**-ser-size/

* *noun* **exercises**
1 an action performed to strengthen the body or
part of the body
I like to do my exercises before I leave for work in
the morning.
2 a piece of work done for practice
There are some exercises given at the end of this book.

* *verb* **exercises, exercising, exercised**
1 If you exercise something, you use it.
He exercised his power over them.

2   If you exercise, you perform some kind of physical activity.
I exercise every day.

3   If you exercise someone or something, you give exercise to them.
I need to exercise the horses.

---

exist /ig-**zist**/ *verb* **exists, existing, existed**

1   If you exist, you are real.
My sister believes that fairies exist.

2   If you exist, you stay alive, often in difficult circumstances.
We had to eat raw potatoes just to exist.

➜   *word family*
existence /ig-**zi**-stense/ *noun*
the act of being real
existent /ig-**zi**-stent/ *adjective*
used to describe something that exists

---

expand /ik-**spand**/ *verb* **expands, expanding, expanded**

1   If something expands, it is made or becomes larger.
These metals expand when heated.

2   If something expands, it spreads out.
His face expanded into a smile.

---

expensive /ik-**spen**-siv/ *adjective*

dear, costing a lot of money
She wears expensive clothes.
He lives in an expensive house.

experience /ik-**spi**-ree-ense/

* *noun* **experiences**

1   a happening in one's own life
    We had a terrible experience in that restaurant.

2   knowledge gained from one's own life or work
    I have lots of experience of working in schools.

* *verb* **experiences, experiencing, experienced**

1   If you experience something, it happens to you.
    Have you experienced the train journey to the north of the country?

2   If you experience something, you feel it.
    I have never experienced such pain before.

expert /**ek**-spert/

* *adjective*
    very skilful and able
    He is an expert tennis player.

* *noun* **experts**
    a person with a special skill or knowledge
    He is an expert in antiques.

➔ *word family*
    expertise /ek-sper-**teez**/ *noun*
    a special skill or knowledge

explore /ik-**sploar**/ *verb* **explores, exploring, explored**

1   If you explore something, you examine it closely.
    Have you explored all the possibilities?

2   If you explore a place or country, you travel all over in order to find out all about it.
    He explored the country for five months.

→ **word family**
exploration /ek-splo-**ray**-shun/ *noun*
the act of exploring
explorer /ik-**splo**-rer/ *noun*
someone who explores distant places

eye /ie/
---
* *noun* **eyes**
the organ we use to see
My eyes are tired after reading for hours.
* *verb* **eyes, eyeing, eyed**
If you eye something, you look at it, or watch it closely.
He was eyeing his friend's cake with envy.
I eyed the policeman warily.

face /fayss/
---
* *noun* **faces**
1   the front part of the head, from the forehead to the chin
She has such a beautiful face.
2   the front part of anything
He fell over and broke the face of his watch.
* *verb* **faces, facing, faced**
1   If you face something, you stand looking towards it.
The house was facing south.
2   If you face something difficult, you meet or encounter it bravely.
They turned to face the enemy.
He must start to face his problems.
3   If you face a surface, you cover it with a different material.
I am going to face the wall with plaster.

fact /**fact**/ *noun* **facts**

1 something known to be true or to have happened
There is a book of geographical facts about the country.

2 the truth
It is a fact that the Earth is round.

3 a deed, an event
It happened after the fact.

fall /**fawl**/

* *verb* **falls, falling**, **fell** /**fel**/, **fallen** /**faw**-len/

1 If you fall, you drop down.
I tripped over a stone and fell.

2 If something falls, it becomes less or lower.
The price of food is falling.

3 If something falls from or to something else, it hangs down.
Her hair fell to her waist.

4 If something falls on a certain day, it happens or occurs then.
The holiday falls on a Sunday.

5 If you fall into a certain state or condition, you enter into it.
I fell asleep as soon as I went to bed.
The room fell silent as the man walked in.

6 If soldiers fall in battle, they are killed.
Many soldiers fell in the war.

* *noun* **falls**

1 a drop or descent
He was badly injured after a fall from the cliff.

2 a lessening or lowering
There has been a fall in the birth rate.

→ *phrases*

If you **fall back**, you go back.

If you **fall on** or **upon** someone, you attack them.

If you **fall out** with someone, you quarrel with them.

If something **falls through**, it fails or does not happen.

---

family /**fam**-lee/ *noun* **families**

1   a household, parents and children
I live in a flat with my family.

2   a person's children and/or spouse
My sister has no family.

→ *usage*

Remember that the word *family* can be used with both a singular or plural verb: **my family has** or **my family have**.

---

farm /**farm**/

∗   *noun* **farms**
an area of land prepared for crops or animals by the owner

∗   *verb* **farms, farming, farmed**
If you farm land, you use it as a farm.
My brother farms the land next to ours.

→ *word family*
farmer /**far**-mer/ *noun*
someone who farms land

→ *phrase*
If you **farm** something **out**, you give it out to be done by others.

fat /**fat**/

*   *adjective* **fatter, fattest**
     well fed, with a lot of flesh on the body
     I used to be quite fat, but am now much thinner.
*   *noun* **fats**
1   an oily substance in animal bodies
     Can you cut the fat off the meat?
2   the oily substance found in animals and in some
     plants, used as a food or in cooking
     The chicken is fried in vegetable fat.

father /**fa**-ther/

*   *noun* **fathers**
1   a male parent
     I am going for dinner tonight with my father.
2   a person who begins, invents, or first makes
     something
     the founding fathers of the United States
*   *verb* **fathers, fathering, fathered**
1   If you father children, you are their father.
     He has fathered several children.
2   If you father an idea or movement, you start it.
     He fathered the Scout movement.
➔   *thesaurus*
     dad, daddy, pa, paw, papa
➔   **word family**
     grandfather, grandad, grandpa *noun*
     your father's father; your mother's father

fear /**feer**/

*   *noun* **fears**
     dread, terror, anxiety
     I have a fear of spiders.
     The noises in the night filled her with fear.

❋ *verb* **fears, fearing, feared**
If you fear something, you are scared of it.
I fear spiders and snakes.

feather /fe-ther/
❋ *noun* **feathers**
one of the long, light growths that cover a bird's body
The bird has beautiful blue-black feathers.
❋ *verb* **feathers, feathering, feathered**
If you feather something, you line or cover it with feathers.
➔ *idiom*
If you **feather your nest**, you make a profit for yourself by taking advantage of a situation.

feeble /fee-bl/ *adjective* **feebler, feeblest**
very weak
The old lady has grown very feeble.
They heard a feeble cry come from the room.
➔ *word family*
feebleness /fee-bil-ness/ *noun*
the state of being feeble

feed /feed/ *verb* **feeds, feeding, fed /fed/**
1 If you feed someone, you give them food to eat.
   I always feed the children an hour before we eat.
2 If you feed, you eat.
   The cats were feeding on mice.
3 If you feed something, you provide what is necessary for it to function.
   Coal feeds the furnace.
   The story will feed their imagination.

4 If you feed something into something else, you put it into it.
Feed the data into the computer.

feel /feel/

✳ *verb* **feels, feeling, felt /felt/**

1 If you feel something, you touch it.
I could feel the bump on his head.

2 If you feel something, you find out about it by touching.
I could feel the quality of the cloth.

3 If you feel an emotion, you experience it or become aware of it.
I felt a sudden anger.

4 If you feel something, you believe or consider it.
I feel that she is too old for the job.

5 If you say you feel for someone, you pity them.
I really do feel for the orphaned children.

✳ *noun*
the sense of touch, a quality as revealed by touch
the smooth feel of silk

➔ *word family*
feeling /fee-ling/ *noun*

1 the sense of touch
She lost the feeling in the fingers of her right hand.

2 emotion
There was a feeling of sadness.

3 kindness or sympathy for others
I have no feeling for the disgraced politician.

4 an impression or belief
I have a feeling that he is lying.

* *adjective*

able to understand the emotions of others

She is a very feeling person.

female /**fee**-male/ *adjective*

1 consisting of or reserved for girls or women

I went into the female changing area.

2 of or relating to the sex that produces offspring

Our female dog is having puppies soon.

fertile /**fer**-tile/ *adjective*

1 able to produce a lot, fruitful

They farm very fertile land.

2 inventive

She has a fertile imagination.

3 able to reproduce or bear offspring

Her medical tests showed that she was fertile.

➔ *word family*

fertility /fer-**ti**-li-tee/ *noun*

the state of being fertile

fiction /**fic**-shun/ *noun*

1 a made-up story

The account of the event was a complete fiction.

2 the art of writing stories

He writes works of fiction.

3 novels

They publish award-winning fiction.

field /**feeld**/

* *noun* **fields**

1 an enclosed area of ground

The horse lives in a great big field.

2 a sports ground
They were playing on the football field.

3 an area of study or expertise
He is an expert in the field of zoology.

✳ *verb* **fields, fielding, fielded**

1 to catch and return a ball
He fielded the ball from the other side of the pitch.

2 to put a team or player in the field for a game
They fielded a very good team for the match.

3 to deal with or handle
The CEO fielded all of the questions from the staff.
I'm fielding phone calls for my colleague when she's in a meeting.

➔ *phrase*
A **field trip** is a trip away from the classroom or workplace to experience and learn something new.

fight /fīte/

✳ *verb* **fights, fighting, fought** /fot/

1 If you fight, you use force against another person.
The boys were fighting.

2 If you fight, you take part in a war or battle.
The armies are fighting.

3 If you fight, you quarrel or argue.
My brother and sister are always fighting.

4 If you fight for something, you try hard to succeed.
He is in hospital, fighting for his life.

✳ *noun* **fights**

1 a struggle in which force is used, a battle
There was a terrible fight last night.

2 a hard effort
It was a fight to stay alive.

find /finde/

* *verb* **finds, finding, found /found/**

1   If you find something, you come upon what you are looking for.
Did you find the lost ring?

2   If you find something, you discover it.
He was too late to find oil.

3   If you find that something is true, you decide it is so.
The jury found the accused guilty.

* *noun* **finds**
a valuable discovery
It was quite a remarkable find.

finger /fing-ger/

* *noun* **fingers**
one of the five points that extend from the hand or a glove
I was pointing my finger at the picture.

* *verb* **fingers, fingering, fingered**
If you finger something, you touch it with your fingers.
I fingered the piano keys.

fire /fire/

* *noun* **fires**
the activity of burning, which gives out heat and light
The villagers were trying to put out the forest fire.

* *verb* **fires, firing, fired**

1   If you fire a gun, you cause a bullet to be shot from it at speed.
She fired a gun at the door.

2 If you fire someone, you dismiss them from employment.

He fired his assistant for being late every day.

fish /fish/

✳ *noun* **fish**

a cold-blooded animal with gills and fins that lives in water

There are lots of fish in the sea.

✳ *verb* **fishes, fishing, fished**

1 If you fish, you try to catch fish from a river or the sea.

He was fishing in the sea.

2 If you fish for something, you search for it.

She was fishing in her bag for her keys.

➔ *usage*

The plural of fish is usually **fish**, rather than **fishes**.

All the fish in the tank were tropical fish.

fix /fiks/ *verb* **fixes, fixing, fixed**

1 If you fix something, you make it firm.

I need to fix the loose tiles.

2 If you fix something that is broken, you repair it.

I tried to fix the broken radio.

3 If you fix something such as a meeting, you arrange it.

I would like to fix a meeting.

4 If you fix something such as a brooch or a hair clip, you fasten it.

She fixed a brooch to her dress.

flag /flag/
* *noun* **flags**
1 a square or oblong piece of material with a pattern on it representing a country, party, association, etc
They flew the French flag.
2 a coloured cloth or paper used as a sign or signal
There are red flags at dangerous beaches.
* *verb* **flags, flagging, flagged**
1 If you flag something, you signal with flags.
The organization flags dangerous beaches.
2 If you flag down a car, you cause it to stop by signalling to the driver.
The police are flagging down speeding motorists.

flame /flame/ *noun* **flames**
a stream of fire, a blaze
She blew out the candle flame.

flat /flat/
* *adjective* **flatter, flattest**
1 level
They cycled along the flat road.
2 uninteresting, dull, and lifeless
Things were a bit flat after Christmas.
3 Music that is flat is below the right note.
The violin was a bit flat.
4 lying full length
People lay flat on the ground after the explosion.
5 deflated, without enough air in it
She had a flat tyre.

6 clear, strong, firm
He gave a flat denial.

7 no longer fizzy
Her sparkling mineral water had gone flat.

✳ *noun* **flats**

1 a level area
I prefer to cycle on the flat.

2 the flat part or side
I slapped him with the flat of my hand.

3 a flat tyre
I went to fix the flat.

4 an apartment
We live in a block of flats.

➜ *word family*
flatness *noun*
the state of being flat

---

flight /**flite**/ *noun* **flights**

1 the act of flying
the flight of the swallow

2 the act of running away, fleeing
the flight from civil war

3 the movement or path of a thing through the air
We watched the flight of the arrow.

4 a journey made by air
I have booked a flight to Paris.

---

fling /**fling**/ *verb* **flings**, **flinging**, **flung** /**flung**/

1 If you fling something, you throw it.
I flung the papers on the floor.

2 If someone flings themselves, they move suddenly and forcefully.
The little boy flung himself onto the floor in a temper.

floor /flore/ *noun* **floors**

1 the bottom surface of a room on which a person walks
She walked across the uncarpeted floor.

2 any bottom surface
The fish lives on the floor of the ocean.

3 all the rooms, etc, on the same level in a building
I rent the first and second floors of the house.

flower /flour/

* *noun* **flowers**

1 a blossom, consisting of petals and bearing pollen
My husband gave me the most beautiful bunch of flowers.

2 the best part of
*The flower of the nation's young men were lost
during the war.*

* *verb* **flowers, flowering, flowered**
If something flowers, it blossoms or blooms.
The daffodils have flowered and look beautiful.

fold /foald/

* *verb* **folds, folding, folded**

1 If you fold something, you bend one part of it all
the way over to cover another part.
I folded the blanket in half.

2 If you fold something in something else, you
enclose it.
He folded her in his arms.

* *noun* **folds**

1 a line or crease made by folding
I tried to iron out the folds in the sheets.

2 the part doubled over
I stuck some money into the fold.

food /**food**/ noun

something that you eat
I'm hungry and would like some food.

→ *usage*
Food isn't usually used in the plural.

fool /**fool**/ noun **fools**

someone who is silly or stupid

→ *word family*
foolish /**foo**-lish/ adjective
silly, stupid
That was a foolish thing to do.

→ *phrases*
If you make a **fool of yourself**, you make yourself
look silly.
If you make a **fool of someone**, you make them
look silly.

foot /**foot**/ noun **feet** /**feet**/

1 the part of the leg below the ankle
I have sore feet after walking the streets all day.
2 the lowest part of anything
I jumped to the foot of the stairs.

forbid /fawr-**bid**/ verb **forbids, forbidding, forbade** /fawr-
bade/, **forbidden** /fawr-**bi**-den/

If you forbid something, you order it not to be done.
He forbade his son to drive his car.

force /**foarse**/

* *noun* **forces**
1 strength, power
The force of the wind is strong.

2 violence
I had to use force to get him into the car.

3 an organized body of people
My brother would like to join the police force.

4 (**forces**) the army, navy, and air force
The military forces are fighting in the war.

5 a person or thing that has great power
He is a force in the local council.

✷ *verb* **forces, forcing, forced**

1 to make somebody do something
Force him to clean his room.

2 to get something by strength, violence, or effort
He had to force his way through the crowd.

---

forecast /**foar**-cast/

✷ *verb* **forecasts, forecasting, forecast**
to say what will happen in the future
It is impossible to forecast the result of the match.
It is easier nowadays to forecast the weather.

✷ *noun* **forecasts**
a statement about what is likely to happen in the future that often refers to the weather
Have you seen the forecast for tomorrow?

➔ *collocation*
*We broadcast an hourly **weather forecast** for the UK and Ireland.*

---

foresee /foar-**see**/ *verb* **foresees, foreseeing, foresaw** /fore-**saw**/, **foreseen** /fore-**seen**/

If you foresee something, you see that it will happen in the future.
No one could have foreseen the accident.

foretell /foar-**tell**/ *verb* **foretells, foretelling, foretold** /foar-**toald**/

If you foretell something, you say that it will happen in the future.

She claims to be able to foretell the future from the stars.

forget /fawr-**get**/ *verb* **forgets, forgetting, forgot** /fawr-**got**/, **forgotten** /fawr-**got**-en/

If you forget something, you fail to remember it.

She forgot his name for a minute.

forgive /fawr-**giv**/ *verb* **forgives, forgiving, forgave** /fawr-**gave**/, **forgiven** /fawr-**giv-en**/

1 If you forgive something, you pardon it.
   I will one day forgive her disloyalty.
2 If you forgive someone, you stop being angry or bitter towards them.
   He forgave his son for crashing the car.

➜ *word family*
   forgiveness /fawr-**giv**-ness/ *noun*
   the act of forgiving
   forgivable /fawr-**gi**-va-bul/ *adjective*
   used to describe something that can be forgiven
   forgiving /fawr-**giv**-ing/ *adjective*
   willing to forgive

fork /**fawrk**/
* *noun* **forks**
1 an instrument with two or more pointed prongs used for digging, eating, etc
   She ate her dinner with a fork and no knife.

2   a place where two roads meet
They met at a fork in the road.

✳ *verb* **forks, forking, forked**
1   If you fork something, you raise or dig it with a fork.
The gardener forked the soil.
2   If something forks, it divides into branches.
The road forks outside the town.

forsake /fawr-**sake**/ *verb* **forsakes, forsaking**, **forsook**
/fawr-**sook**/, **forsaken** /fawr-**say**-ken/

If you forsake something, you give it up.
He forsook his family for the sake of his love.

forward /**fawr**-wurd/

✳ *adverb*
towards the front
They tried to step forward.

✳ *adjective*
1   advancing
He made a forward movement.
2   near the front
He moved towards the forward part of the bus.
3   in advance
I have finished my forward planning for the week.
4   developing more quickly than usual
She is very forward for her age.
5   upfront or impolite
She was very forward about asking for more money.

✳ *verb* **forwards, forwarding, forwarded**
If you forward something, you send it on.
Please forward my mail to my new address.

129

free /**free**/

✱ *adjective* **freer, freest**

1   at liberty, able to do what a person wants
    In the afternoons she is free to amuse herself.
    The animals on the farm are free to wander.

2   not forced or persuaded to act, think, speak, etc,
    in a particular way
    We have the right to free speech.

3   not occupied
    There are rooms free in the hotel.

4   generous
    He is very free with his money.

5   costing nothing
    The goods are given free.

6   open, frank
    He has a free manner.

✱ *verb* **frees, freeing, freed**

1   If you free someone, you set them at liberty.
    They are thinking of freeing the prisoner.

2   If you free something, you liberate it from
    something else.
    This freed him from his responsibility.

freeze /**freez**/ *verb* **freezes, freezing, froze** /**froze**/**, frozen**
/**fro**-zen/

1   If you freeze something, you cause it to become
    hard by exposing it to extreme cold.
    Freeze the soup in batches.

2   If something freezes, it becomes or is made into ice.
    The pond sometimes freezes during winter.

3   If you are freezing, you are very cold.
    I am freezing today.

4   If you freeze, you become suddenly still.
He froze when he saw the gunman.

frequent

＊   *adjective* /**free**-kwent/
happening often, common
He is a frequent visitor to the house.

＊   *verb* /free-**kwent**/ **frequents, frequenting, frequented**
If you frequent somewhere, you visit it often.
I frequent the store at the corner.

front /**frunt**/ *noun* **fronts**

the forward part of anything
The front of the building is stone.

fruit /**froot**/ *noun*

1   the part of a plant that produces the seed, often eaten as a food
We have apples, pears, and other fruits.

2   result
He presented the fruits of his research.

fun /**fun**/

＊   *noun* **fun**
An activity is fun if it is enjoyable and makes people feel happy.
Everyone joined in the fun.

＊   *adjective*
enjoyable
It was a fun evening.

funny /**fun**-ee/ *adjective* **funnier, funniest**

used to describe someone or something that makes us laugh

The joke was very funny.

→ *usage*

Fun and **funny** should not be confused. Something fun is enjoyable, but it does not necessarily make you laugh.

future /**fyoo**-cher/

* *adjective*

about to happen, coming

future projects

* *noun* **future**

the time to come

In the future we will take more care.

garden /**gar**-den/

* *noun* **gardens**

a piece of land on which flowers or vegetables are grown

I like to sit in the garden and look at the flowers.

* *verb* **gardens, gardening, gardened**

If you garden, you look after a garden, often as a hobby.

I would like to find time to garden.

→ *word family*

gardener /**gar**-de-ner/ *noun*

someone who gardens

gardening /**gard**-ning/ *noun*

the act of attending to a garden

Gardening is hard work.

general /**je**-ne-ral/ *adjective*

1   including every one of something
    There has been a general lowering of prices throughout the industry.

2   not specialized
    He has very good general knowledge.

3   common, usual, normal
    Try and follow the general procedure.

4   taken as a whole, overall
    The invalid still has a weak arm but her general condition is good.

5   not detailed
    Could you give us a general description of the man?

get /**get**/ *verb* **gets, getting** /**ge**-ting/, **got** /**got**/

1   If you get something, you obtain it.
    I need to get some money.

2   If you get somewhere, you reach it.
    We'll get there in time if the bus comes soon.

3   If you get into a particular state, you become it.
    I am getting older.

girl /**girl**/ *noun* **girls**

1   a female child
    She had a baby girl on Tuesday.

2   a young woman
    Have you asked the girls if they want to come to the cinema?

3   a daughter
    They have two boys and a girl.

→ *word family*
girlfriend /**girl**-frend/ *noun*

1 a female friend
She is having lunch with her girlfriends.

2 a female romantic partner
He is out on a date with his girlfriend.

girlish /**gir**-lish/ *adjective*
like or of a girl
He heard the sound of girlish laughter.

give /giv/ **verb** **gives, giving, gave** /gave/, **given** /**gi**-ven/

1 If you give someone a present, you hand it to
them and it is for them to keep.
I gave him a book for his birthday.

2 If you give something to someone, you hand it
over to them.
Give the money to the bank.

3 You can use give to mean allow.
He was given a chance to tell us his idea.

4 If you give a noise or movement, you make
it.
He gave a shout.

5 Give can also mean produce
Cows give milk.

6 If you give a party, you organize it.
We give a party every New Year.

7 If something gives, it yields, bends, or
breaks.
The heavy door gave under pressure.

→ *word family*
giver /**gi**-ver/ *noun*
someone who gives something

→ *phrases*

If you **give** something **away**, you give it as a gift, or you tell something that is secret.

If you **give ground**, you go backwards.

If you **give in**, you admit defeat.

If you **give** something **up** for someone, you leave it to be taken by them.

If you **give** something **up**, you stop it.

If you **give up hope**, you lose hope.

If you **give way**, you stop in order to allow someone or something to pass.

---

glass /glass/

---

* *noun* **glasses**

1   a hard, easily broken transparent material
The door is made of glass.

2   a mirror
Look at your reflection in the glass.

3   a glass drinking vessel
She gave him a glass of milk.

* *adjective*
used to describe something that is made of glass

→ *word family*

glasses /gla-siz/ *plural noun*
a pair of lenses set in a frame resting on the nose and ears, used to improve the wearer's eyesight, or to protect the eyes from strong sunlight

---

glove /gluv/ noun gloves

---

a covering of cloth, wool, or leather for the hand, each finger being separately covered
My gloves are wet from throwing snowballs.

go /go/

* *verb* **goes, going, went** /went/, **gone** /gon/

1   If you go somewhere, you travel or move there.
   I went to see my parents over Christmas.
   I was hoping to go to Amsterdam for the weekend.

2   If you go somewhere to do something, you move
   or travel to do it.
   I go to school in the middle of town.

3   If you go something, you become it.
   I thought I was going to go mad.
   I went white-haired with age.

→ **phrases**
   If you **go for** someone, you attack them.
   If you **go in for** something, you take an interest in it.
   If something such as a business **goes under**, it fails.
   If you **have a go at** someone, you attack them verbally.

* **noun**
   Informally, **a go** is a turn at or a chance to do
   something.
   Can I have a go on the new computer?

→ **word family**
   go-ahead /go-a-hed/

* *adjective*
   ready to try out new ideas
   a go-ahead firm

* *noun*
   permission to proceed
   the go-ahead for the new road

goat /goat/ *noun* **goats**

an animal with horns, related to the sheep
Goats often live wild in the mountains.

gold /**goald**/ *noun*

1 a precious metal
My wedding ring is made of gold.

2 wealth, money
The man was counting his gold.

3 the colour of gold
She wore gold shoes.

➔ **word family**

golden /**goal**-den/ *adjective*

1 made of gold
She wore golden rings on her finger.

2 of the colour of gold
He had golden locks of hair.

3 valuable
This job is a golden opportunity.

good /**good**/ *adjective*

1 right, morally acceptable, virtuous
a good deed

2 of a high quality
a good performance
good eyesight

3 pleasant, agreeable, welcome
good news

4 fit, competent
a good teacher

5 well-behaved
Tell the children to be good.

6 kindly
the good fairy in the story

7 clever, talented
good at maths

→ *usage*
Good is an adjective and not an adverb. You should never say that you are **doing good**. Instead say that you are **doing well**.

government /**gu**-ver-ment/ *noun* **governments**
1 the act or way of ruling
The country runs on a democratic system of government.
2 the group of people who direct the affairs of a country
Three ministers have resigned from the government.
→ *word family*
governmental /gu-ver-**men**-tal/ *adjective*
relating to government

grain /**grane**/ *noun* **grains**
1 a seed of wheat, corn, etc
I eat wholemeal bread with grains for breakfast.
2 a very small hard particle
a grain of salt
3 a very small amount
She told me there was not a grain of truth in the story.
4 the pattern of markings in wood, leather, etc
There was a very pretty grain in the wood.

grass /**grass**/ *noun*
a plant that commonly covers the ground, usually green
We planted grass at the front of the garden.
→ *word family*
grassy *adjective*
covered in grass

green /**green**/

* *adjective*
1 of the colour of grass
   She was wearing a green dress.
2 concerned with the protection and conservation of the environment
   The politicians were discussing green issues.

* *noun* **greens**
1 a green colour
   She always wears green.
2 a piece of ground covered with grass
   The children were playing cricket on the village green.
3 a person or group who is concerned with the protection and conservation of the environment
   I'm supporting the greens at the election.

➔ *word family*
   greens /**greenz**/ *plural noun*
   green vegetables, for example, spinach
   We told the children to eat their greens.
   greenery /**green**-ree/ *noun*
   green plants, foliage
   My mother arranged the flowers in a vase with some greenery.
   greenhouse /**green**-house/ *noun*
   a glasshouse for growing plants
   I grow tomatoes in a greenhouse.

grey /**gray**/, *also* **gray** /**gray**/ *adjective*

1 black mixed with white in colour
   a grey dress
2 of the colour of hair whitened by age
   grey hair

139

grind /grinde/ *verb* **grinds, grinding, ground** /ground/

1 If you grind something, you rub or crush it to powder or small pieces.
I ground the coffee before breakfast.

2 If you grind something to make it sharp, you rub it against something else.
I ground the knives against a special stone to sharpen them.

3 If you grind things together, you press them together noisily.
He's been grinding his teeth in his sleep.

grip /grip/

∗ *verb* **grips, gripping** /gri-ping/, **gripped** /gript/

1 If you grip something, you take a firm hold of it, or hold it very tightly.
The child gripped his mother's hand.

2 If you grip someone's attention, you seize it and keep it on you.
The audience was gripped by the play.

∗ *noun* **grips**
a firm or tight hold
He kept a tight grip on his wallet.

group /groop/

∗ *noun* **groups**

1 a number of people or things taken together
a group of teenagers

2 a set of people who play music or sing together
They are my favourite pop group.

* *verb* **groups, grouping, grouped**
If you group things, you put them together into a group.
Group the books according to subject.
I try not to group the children in the class according to ability.

grow /gro/ *verb* **grows, growing, grew /groo/, grown /groan/**

1 If you grow, you become bigger or taller.
The children are growing quickly.
2 If plants grow, they have life.
I would like plants that can grow in any soil.
3 If you grow to be something, you become it.
My parents are growing old.
4 If you grow plants or flowers, you plant and rear them.
I'm thinking about growing potatoes in the back garden.

➔ *word family*
growth /groath/ *noun*
1 the act of growing
2 something that has grown

guide /gide/

* *verb* **guides, guiding, guided**
1 If you guide someone, you lead them to the place they want to go.
I will guide them up the mountain.
2 If you are guided by something, you are influenced by it.
Try and be guided by your common sense.

* *noun* **guides**

1 a person who shows the way
   He spent the summer as a mountain guide.

2 a person who directs or influences someone's behaviour
   His father was also his guide and friend.

3 a person who leads people around a place, pointing out things of interest
   The guide took tourists around the castle.

4 a thing that helps one to form an opinion or make a calculation
   Use this year's sales as a guide to the firm's financial situation.

→ *word family*
   guidance /**gie**-danse/ *noun*
   help and advice
   I was hoping to get career guidance.

gun /**gun**/ *noun* **guns**

any weapon that fires bullets or shells by means of explosive
A loaded gun was found near the crime scene.

hair /**hair**/ *noun* **hairs**

any or all of the thread-like growths covering the skin of humans and animals
She had pretty long dark hair.

→ *phrase*
   If you **split hairs**, you point out differences so slight that they could be overlooked.

→ *word family*
   hairless /**hair**-less/ *adjective*
   without any hair

hairy /**hay**-ree/ *adjective*
with hair

hairbrush /**hair**-brush/ *noun*
a brush for grooming the hair

haircut /**hair**-cut/ *noun*
a cutting of the hair of the head or the style in which this is done

hairdo /**hair**-do/ *noun*
the style in which hair is arranged
She had a new hairdo for the party.

hairdresser /**hair**-dre-ser/ *noun*
a person who cuts and styles hair as a job
I have an appointment with my hairdresser to get my hair washed and trimmed.

→ *usage*
Remember that when you refer to all of the hair on your head, you say **hair** rather than **hairs**.

hammer /**ham**-er/

∗ *noun* **hammers**
1 a tool for pounding nails, beating metal, etc
I needed a hammer and some nails to build a chest.
2 a part of a machine or a device that strikes
the hammers in a piano

∗ *verb* **hammers**, **hammering**, **hammered**
1 If you hammer something, you use a hammer to drive or beat it.
I tried to hammer the nail into the wall.
2 If you hammer at something, you strike it hard.
Police were hammering at the door.

hand /hand/

* *verb* **hands, handing, handed**

If you hand someone something, you give it to them with your hand.

I handed him the book.

* *noun* **hands**

1 the end of the arm below the wrist

My hands are very cold.

2 a worker

He worked as a factory hand.

3 the cards given to one player in a card game

I hope I've been dealt a good hand in this game.

4 the pointer of a clock or watch

The minute hand of the clock was broken.

5 a share, a part, an influence

I suspect he had a hand in the robbery.

→ *phrases*

If you are **hand in glove with** someone, you are close to them and possibly involved in some wrongdoing with them.

If you live **hand-to-hand with** someone, you live at close quarters with them.

If you live **hand-to-mouth,** you have just enough money to live on with nothing for the future.

If something is **out of hand,** it is out of control.

If someone has the **upper hand in** a situation, they have control.

If you **wash your hands of** something, you refuse to have anything more to do with it.

If you **give someone a hand** you assist them in doing something.

hang /hang/ *verb* **hangs, hanging, hung** /hung/

1 If you hang something, you fix one part of it up on something and allow the rest to drop.
I am going to hang the picture from a hook.

2 If something hangs, it goes down and reaches down.
She hung her head in shame.
Her hair was hanging down her back.

→ *usage*
Hanged is only used in the past tense when referring to a person who has been executed. Otherwise it is **hung.**

happy /**ha**-pee/ *adjective* **happier, happiest**

1 pleased, full of joy
She was really happy to see him.

2 lucky
They met by a happy chance.

3 pleasant, joyful
The wedding was an extremely happy occasion.

→ *word family*
happiness /**ha**-pee-ness/ *noun*
the state of being happy

harbour /**har**-bur/

✳ *noun* **harbours**

1 a sheltered place where ships and boats are kept
We walked down to the harbour to see the moored boats.

2 a place of shelter
They regarded his house as a harbour from the weather.

✳ *verb* **harbours, harbouring, harboured**

1 If you harbour someone, you give them shelter.
   It is against the law to harbour criminals.

2 If you harbour an emotion, you hold it privately.
   She harboured a grudge against her former friend.

hard /hard/

✳ *adjective* **harder, hardest**

1 firm, solid
   The nut has a hard shell.

2 difficult
   It was a hard task but I tried to do it anyway.

3 unfeeling, unkind, cruel
   He was a hard boss.
   She gave her mother a hard look.

4 harsh, severe
   We thought he was given a hard punishment.
   He has had a hard life.

✳ *adverb*

1 with force
   He hit the nail hard with his hammer.
   He was hit hard on the head by the falling debris.
   It was raining hard last night.

2 with great effort
   She works very hard.

3 close
   The dog followed hard on his heels.

4 with great attention
   She stared hard and long at the picture.

➜ *phrases*
   If you are **hard of hearing**, you are quite deaf.
   If you are **hard up,** you have little money.

harmony /**har**-mo-nee/ *noun* **harmonies**

1   agreement, friendship
They used to be enemies but now they live in harmony.

2   the pleasant effect made by parts combining into a whole
The harmony of colours in the garden was quite beautiful.

3   the playing or singing at one time of musical notes that are pleasant when sounded together
The two girls sing in perfect harmony.

hat /**hat**/ *noun* **hats**

a head covering
You should wear a hat as it's cold outside.

hate /**hate**/

✷   *verb* **hates, hating, hated**
If you hate something or someone, you dislike it or them greatly.
He hates his job.

✷   *noun* **hates**
a great dislike
He is full of hate for his rival.

➜   *phrase*
A **hate crime** is crime against a person that has been committed because of race, religion, gender, etc.

➜   *word family*
hateful /**hate**-fool/ *adjective*
deserving or causing hate
a hateful job/a hateful person.
hatred /**hate**-red/ *noun*
great dislike
He looked at his rival with hatred.

have /**hav**/ *verb* **has, having, had**

1 If you have something, you possess, own, or hold it.
   He has a fast car.
   I have a book.
   They have the best intentions.

2 If you have to do something, you are forced to do it.
   He has to leave town tomorrow.

→ *phrase*
   If you **have something to do with** something, you
   are involved in it.

he /**hee**/ *pronoun*

   referring to a male person or animal
   He went to buy some flowers for his girlfriend.

→ *word family*
   him *pronoun*
   referring to a male person or animal
   The flowers were bought by him.
   himself *pronoun*
   reflexive form of **he**
   John bought the flowers for himself.
   his *determiner*
   associated with **him**
   The flowers are his, not hers.

head /**hed**/

* *noun* **heads**

1 the top part of the body
   I bumped my head on the table.

2 a person's mind
   He has a good head.

3 the chief person in a group
   He has got a job as head of the department.

4 the top or front part
I'd like to get to the head of the line.

✳ *verb* **heads, heading, headed**

1 If you head somewhere, you go towards it.
We headed out to the farm.

2 If you head something, you lead or direct it.
He heads the London office.

3 If you head a ball, you hit it with your head.
He headed the ball back to the goalkeeper.

---

healthy /**helth**-ee/ *adjective* **healthier, healthiest**

1 having good health
She is a healthy young woman.

2 causing good health
It is a healthy climate in which to live.
He has a healthy diet.

---

hear /**heer**/ *verb* **hears, hearing, heard** /**herd**/

1 If you hear, you perceive sounds by the ear.
I can hear birdsong in the mornings.

2 If you hear something, you listen to it.
You should wait and hear what they have to say.

➜ *word family*
hearing /**hee**-ring/ *noun*

1 the ability to hear sounds
My dog has very sharp hearing.

2 the distance at which a person can hear
I didn't want to talk about him within his daughter's hearing.

3 the examining of evidence by a judge
We are due to go to court for a hearing.

➜ *phrase*
If you can't hear well, you are **hard of hearing.**

heart /**hart**/ *noun* **hearts**

1   the organ that keeps the blood flowing through the body
    My grandfather suffered from heart disease.

2   the central or most important part of anything
    There is a clearing at the heart of the forest.
    There are fewer shops than there used to be at the heart of the town.

3   the centre of a person's thoughts and emotions
    He knew in his heart that he was dying.

4   a thing shaped like a heart.
    He gave her a valentine's card with hearts on it.

→ *phrases*
    If you **learn something by heart**, you memorize it.
    If you **take something to heart**, you feel deeply about it.

→ *word family*
    heartache /**har**-take/ *noun*
    sorrow
    the heartache of losing a child
    heart attack /**hart** a-**tack**/ *noun*
    a sudden, painful, sometimes fatal medical condition in which the heart stops working normally
    He died of a heart attack.

heat /**heet**/

∗   *noun* **heats**

1   hotness, warmth
    He felt the heat of the sun against his face.

2   anger, excitement
    He stormed out of the house in the heat of the moment.

3 a division of a race from which the winners go on to the final
We are in the final heat of the race.

✱ *verb* **heats, heating, heated**
If you heat something, you make it become warm or hot.
He lit a small fire to heat a large room.

➔ *word family*
heated /**hee**-ted/ *adjective*

1 hot
A heated towel was provided for each dinner guest.

2 angry
They had a heated argument.

heater /**hee**-ter/ *noun*
a device for heating a room, car, water, etc
I turned the heating on as the room was very cold.

---

hide /**hide**/

✱ *verb* **hides, hiding, hid** /**hid**/, **hidden** /**hi**-den/

1 If you hide something, you put or keep it out of sight.
We are trying to hide the presents from the children.

2 If you hide a secret, an emotion, or a feeling, you do not let anybody know about it.
She found it hard to hide her disappointment.

✱ *noun* **hides**
a camouflaged place used by bird-watchers, hunters, etc
They had a lovely view over the wetland from the hide.

---

history /**hi**-sto-ree/ *noun* **histories**

1 the study of past events
We studied European history in school.

151

2   an account of past events, conditions, ideas, etc
He told the younger man his life history.

---

hit /hit/

---

*   *verb* **hits**, **hitting** /hi-ting/, **hit**

1   If you hit something or someone, you strike it or them.
I hit the ball with the bat.

2   If you hit a situation, you reach or arrive at it.
He hit a bad patch last year, but is doing much better now.

*   *noun* **hits**

1   a blow
I received a hit over the head.

2   a success
The show was a resounding hit with the critics.

---

hold /hoald/

---

*   *verb* **holds**, **holding**, **held** /held/

1   If you hold something, you have or take it in your hands or arms.
I held the newborn baby carefully.

2   If something holds something else, it carries the weight of it.
The bridge wouldn't hold all of the cars.

3   If something holds something, it contains it.
The jug holds a litre of liquid.

4   If you hold a feeling or opinion, you have it.
He holds the view that all people are equal.

5   If you hold something such as a meeting, you cause it to take place.
We are holding a meeting on Thursday evening.

*   *noun* **holds**
grasp
The roads were icy, and I grabbed a firm hold of the wheel.

→ *phrases*

If you **hold forth**, you speak in public or at length.
If you **hold** a shop **up**, you attack and rob it.
If you **hold** something **up,** you delay or hinder it.
If you **hold with** something, you agree with it.
If you **hold your own in** a fight or argument, you keep advantages without gaining any more.
If you **hold back**, you show restraint, or refrain from doing something.

hole /hole/ *noun* **holes**

1   a hollow or empty space in something solid
I lost a wheel driving through a hole in the road.
2   an opening
The cows got out through a hole in the fence.
3   a difficulty
We've found ourselves in a bit of a financial hole.

hollow /hol-o/

∗ *adjective*
1   not solid, with a hole inside
The tree was hollow.
2   not sincere
I felt his promises were hollow as he'd let us down before.
∗ *noun* **hollows**
1   a sunken place, something hollow
He had hollows in the cheeks.
2   a depression or dip in the land
There was mist lying in the hollow.
→ *phrase*
If you **hollow something out**, you empty it or make a hole in it.
He hollowed out the coconut.

hook /hook/

∗ *noun* **hooks**

a piece of metal or plastic bent for catching hold of things or for hanging things on

There's a hook on the bathroom door for towels.

Attach a fish hook to the end of the fishing line.

∗ *verb* **hooks, hooking, hooked**

If you hook something, you catch, hold, or fasten it with a hook.

He hooked a large salmon on his fishing trip.

➔ *phrase*

If you do something **by hook or by crook,** you do it by any means, fair or unfair.

If you are **hooked by** something, it has greatly caught your attention.

If you are **hooked on** something, you are addicted to it.

hope /hope/

∗ *verb* **hopes, hoping, hoped**

If you hope for something, you wish for it or expect to get it in the future.

He hopes for better things.

∗ *noun* **hopes**

a wish or expectation for the future

She has hopes of going to university next year.

➔ *word family*

hopeful /hope-ful/ *adjective*

1 full of hope

She was in a hopeful mood.

2 giving cause for hope

There are hopeful signs that he will make a full recovery.

hopeless /**hope**-less/ *adjective*

1   without hope
They felt utterly hopeless about the situation.

2   giving no cause for hope
This is a hopeless cause.

3   poor, not good
Despite attending classes she is still a hopeless cook.

horn /**horn**/ *noun* **horns**

1   a hard, pointed growth on the heads of some animals
The bull had enormous horns.

2   a musical brass instrument
My brother plays the French horn.

3   an instrument on a vehicle that makes a warning noise
He beeped his horn at the car in front.

horse /**horss**/ *noun* **horses**

1   an animal that can be used for riding on or pulling loads
There are three horses in the field.

2   a device or frame with legs to support something
I hung my wet clothes to dry on the clothes horse.

3   a padded block on four legs used by gymnasts in vaulting
His complicated vault on the horse won him a medal.

hospital /**hos**-pi-tal/ *noun* **hospitals**

a building for the care of sick or injured people
I had to go to hospital after the accident.

➜   *word family*

hospitalization /hos-pi-ta-lie-**zay**-shun/ *noun*
the act of being put into a hospital for a time

hour /our/ noun hours

1 60 minutes
It took us two hours to find the house.

2 the time fixed for doing something, the time at which something is usually done
Can you do the work within business hours?

house

∗ *noun* /**howss**/ houses

1 a building in which people can live; a home

2 an establishment
a publishing house

➔ *collocation*
The restaurant's **house red** *is very good.*
The book was produced **in-house**.

➔ *Phrase*
If something is **on the house** it is free.

∗ *verb* /**howz**/ houses, housing, housed

1 If something is housed somewhere, it is in or kept in that place.
The watch was housed in a silver case.

2 If someone is housed they are given a home.
The refugees were housed in rented accommodation.

humour /**hyoo**-mur/ noun

1 a comical or amusing quality
I can't see the humour in that rude comment.

2 a state of mind, mood
He is in a good humour today.

➔ *collocation*
She has a great **sense of humour**.

➔ *word family*
humorous /**hyoo**-mu-rus/ *adjective*

1 funny, amusing

He told us a very humorous story.

2 having or displaying a sense of humour

She is a very humorous person.

hurt /hurt/ *verb* **hurts, hurting, hurt**

1 If you hurt someone or something, you cause them or it pain.

He hurt his hand on broken glass.

2 If you hurt someone's feelings, you upset them.

He was hurt by his brother's remarks.

➔ *word family*

hurtful /**hurt**-ful/ *adjective*

causing someone to feel upset

She was upset by her friend's hurtful remarks.

I /eye/ *pronoun. See also* **me** *and* **you**

referring back to the speaker or writer

I was the first person here.

ice /eyess/

✱ *noun*

frozen water

He slipped on the ice outside the house.

✱ *verb* **ices, icing, iced**

1 If you ice something you chill it with ice.

I am icing the injury to bring the swelling down.

2 If you ice a cake you cover it with a paste made from powdered sugar.

I watched him ice the birthday cake for his daughter.

➔ *idiom*

If you **break the ice**, you make people you have just met feel more comfortable.

I told a joke to break the ice.

idea /eye-**dee**-ya/ noun **ideas**

1 a plan, thought, or suggestion
   I have an idea for a book.
2 a picture in the mind
   They seem to have an idea of the design they want.
3 an opinion or belief
   She has very strong political ideas.

ill /ill/ adjective

sick, not healthy
The patients in this hospital ward are very ill.

➔ *usage*
You say **seriously** or **very ill**, but not **badly ill**.

impulse /**im**-pulse/ noun **impulses**

a sudden desire or decision to act at once
She bought the new dress on impulse.

➔ *word family*
impulsive /im-**pul**-siv/ adjective
1 done without thought beforehand
   It was an impulsive decision to buy an expensive bike.
2 acting without thinking first
   He is a very impulsive young man.

increase /in-**creess**/

✱ verb **increases, increasing, increased**
   If something increases, it becomes greater in size or number.
   The number of club members has increased.
   The temperature has increased this week.
✱ noun /**in**-creess/ **increases**
   a rise in amount, number, or degree
   a sharp increase in club membership
   There has been an increase in temperature this week.

incredible /in-**cre**-di-bul/ *adjective*

1 unbelievable, hard to believe
   I find his story completely incredible.

2 amazing, wonderful
   It was an incredible performance.

industry /in-du-stree/ *noun* **industries**

in trade or commerce, the work that is done to make goods ready for selling, the manufacturing and selling of goods
There is a thriving industry in the city.

→ *word family*
industrious /in-**du**-stree-us/ *adjective*
hard-working, busy, skilful, clever
The industrious children were studying for their exams.

ink /ingk/ *noun* **inks**

a coloured liquid used for writing or printing
The computer has run out of ink.

insect /in-sect/ *noun* **insects**

any of a large group of small creatures that have a body divided into three sections, six legs, and usually wings

instrument /in-stru-ment/ *noun* **instruments**

1 a tool, especially one used for delicate work
   The surgical instruments were sterilized.

2 a device producing musical sound
   The violin is a stringed instrument.

3 a device for measuring, recording, controlling, etc, especially in an aircraft
   The pilot checked all the flight instruments.

→ *word family*
instrumental /in-stru-**men**-tal/ *adjective*

1 being the cause of
She was instrumental in getting him hired.

2 played on musical instruments
I like listening to instrumental music rather than singing.

insure /in-**shoor**/ *verb* **insures, insuring, insured**

If you insure something, you pay regular sums to a society on condition that you receive an agreed amount of money in case of loss, accident, death, etc
We have insured the house against fire and flood.

→ *word family*
insurance /in-**shoo**-ranse/ *noun*

the arrangement in which you pay money to insure something
We have car and house insurance.

interest /**in**-trest/

* *noun* **interests**

1 something in which a person takes part eagerly
His main interests are tennis and football.

2 advantage
It was in his interest to agree to the proposal.

3 eager attention
He gave the matter all his interest.

4 concern
This problem is of interest to all of us.

5 the money paid for the use of a loan of money
The rate of interest on his bank loan is increasing.

* *verb* **interests, interesting, interested**

If something interests you, it gains your attention.
His books really interest me.

→ **word family**
interesting /**in**-tres-ting/ *adjective*
arousing interest
That is very interesting information.

→ **usage**
Remember that there is a difference between
interested and **interesting**. You feel interested
when something is interesting.

---

invent /in-**vent**/ *verb* **invents, inventing, invented**

1 If you invent something, you think of and plan
   something new.
   He would like to invent a completely new kind of camera.

2 If you invent a story, you make it up.
   She invented a story about her car breaking down.

→ **word family**
inventor /in-**ven**-tor/ *noun*
someone who thinks of and plans something new
He was the inventor of a new app.
invention /in-**ven**-shun/ *noun*

1 a thing thought of and made for the first time
   The telephone was one of his inventions.

2 the ability to think out new ideas
   He admired her powers of invention.
   inventive /in-**ven**-tiv/ *adjective*
   good at thinking of new or unusual ideas
   She was a particularly inventive writer.

---

iron /**eye**-urn/

* *noun* **irons**

1 a common metal, used in construction and
   engineering
   The bridge is made of iron.

2   a tool or instrument, formerly made of iron,
     especially for smoothing clothes
     They bought a new steam iron.

*   *adjective*
1   made of iron
     The park is surrounded by iron railings.
2   strong, hard
     She has an iron will and won't do something she
     doesn't want to.

*   *verb* **irons, ironing, ironed**
     If you iron clothes, you smooth them with an
     iron.
     She hated ironing shirts.

→   *idioms*
     If you **have too many irons in the fire**, you try to do
     too many things at once.
     If you **strike while the iron is hot**, you act at the
     most opportune moment.

---

island /**eye**-land/ *noun* **islands**

     a piece of land surrounded by water
     He dreamt of living on a desert island.

→   *word family*
     islander /**eye**-lan-der/ *noun*
     a native of an island
     The islanders joined together for a dance.

---

jacket /**ja**-ket/ *noun* **jackets**

1   a short coat
     There's a man's woollen jacket in the sale.
2   a loose paper cover for a book
     The book has a striking design on its jacket.

jail /jale/ *noun* **jails**

> a prison
> *The man was sentenced and sent to jail.*

jam¹ /jam/ *noun* **jams**

> fruit boiled with sugar to preserve it
> *I like to eat toast with strawberry jam.*

jam² /jam/

* *verb* **jams, jamming** /ja-ming/, **jammed** /jamd/
1   If you jam something, you squeeze it in somewhere so tightly that movement is impossible.
> *He jammed his foot in the doorway.*
2   If people jam a place, they fill it completely.
> *Protesters jammed the hall.*
* *noun* **jams**
> a lot of traffic in one place so that it takes a long time to get through
> *There are bad traffic jams in the town during rush hour.*

jewel /joo-ul, jool/ *noun* **jewels**

1   a precious stone
> *diamonds, emeralds, and other jewels*
2   something valued highly
> *The painting is the jewel of his art collection.*
➜   **word family**
> **jeweller** /joo-u-ler/ *noun*
> someone who buys and sells jewellery

jewellery /joo-ul-ree, joo-lu-ree/ *noun*

> personal ornaments, as rings, necklaces, bracelets, etc, often decorated with jewels

job /**job**/ *noun* **jobs**

1 a piece of work
   He made a good job of mending the table.
2 someone's employment
   She has a job in an office.

join /**join**/

✳ *verb* **joins, joining, joined**
1 If you join things together, you put or fasten them together.
   I'm trying to join the two pieces of string.
2 If you join something, you take part in it with others.
   We joined the search for the missing cow.
3 If you join a place or club, you become a member of it.
   I have joined the local golf club.
✳ *noun* **joins**
   a place where things join
   It is impossible to see the join in the wallpaper.

joke /**joke**/

✳ *noun* **jokes**
   something said or done to cause laughter
   His speech was full of funny jokes.
✳ *verb* **jokes, joking, joked**
   If you joke, you say something to cause laughter.

journey /**jur**-nee/

✳ *noun* **journeys**
   a distance travelled, especially over land
   The trip involved several long journeys by train and bus.
✳ *verb* **journeys, journeying, journeyed**

If you journey somewhere, you travel there.
We journeyed for three days.

→ *usage*

If you visit somewhere and come back again, you call this **a trip**. The **journey** is what you do to get there, and get back again.

---

judge /judge/

* *noun* **judges**

1 someone who presides in a court of law giving advice on matters of law and deciding on the punishment for guilty people
The judge sentenced him to two years in prison.

2 someone who is able to distinguish what is good from what is bad
She is a good judge of wine.
He is a terrible judge of character.

* *verb* **judges, judging, judged**

1 If you judge something or someone, you give an opinion on it.
We judged the school by its exam results.
The jury judged him to be guilty.

2 If you judge a competition, you decide who or what is the best.
She was asked to judge the singing competition.
Is it good or bad? You can be the judge.

3 If you judge someone, you criticize or blame them.
He is quick to judge others.
Don't judge me.

→ *word family*
judgment /**judge**-ment/ *noun*

1 act or power of judging
   His judgment is not to be trusted.
2 the decision given at the end of a law case
3 good sense
   a business decision showing poor judgment
4 an opinion
   In my judgment he is a good player.

jump /jump/
---

* *verb* **jumps, jumping, jumped**
1 If you jump, you push off the ground with your
   feet so that your whole body moves through the air.
   The dog jumped over the wall.
2 If you jump at a noise, you make a sudden quick
   movement in fright.
   He jumped when the door banged.
* *noun* **jumps**
1 a leap
   a parachute jump
2 a sudden, quick movement
3 an obstacle to be jumped over
   My horse fell at the third jump in the race.
→ ***word family***
   jumper /**jum**-per/ *noun*
1 someone who jumps
2 a piece of clothing, often made of wool, that you
   wear on the upper part of your body
→ *phrases*
   If you **jump at** something, you accept it willingly,
   and hastily.
   If you **jump to conclusions**, you believe things to be
   true without waiting for them to be proved so.

keen /keen/ adjective keener, keenest

1 sharp
   She is very clever, with a keen mind.
2 eager, very interested
   keen on cooking
→ *word family*
   keenness /keen-ness/ noun
   the quality of being keen

keep /keep/ verb keeps, keeping, kept /kept/

1 If you keep something, you have it without being required to give it back.
   I told the shop assistant to keep the change.
2 If you keep something, you do not give or throw it away.
   I'd like to keep the old family photographs.
   Can you keep a secret?
3 If you keep in a certain state, you remain in it.
   Please keep calm.
4 If you keep doing something, you continue to do it.
   I kept walking up the hill.
5 If you keep something for someone, you look after it.
   Can you keep my watch for me while I go swimming?
6 If you keep someone, you look after them.
   He was struggling to keep his family.
7 If you keep a date or an engagement, you carry it out.
   Remember to keep our date on Friday.
→ *phrase*
   If you **keep at** something, you go on trying to do it.

→ *idiom*
If you **keep your hand in at** something, you practise it enough to remain good at it.

→ *word family*
keeping /**kee**-ping/ *noun*
care, charge
You should put your documents into your lawyer's keeping.

---

kettle /**ke**-tul/ *noun* **kettles**

a metal vessel, with a spout and handle, used for boiling water
I boiled the kettle to make some tea.

→ *collocation*
Put the kettle on *for a cup of tea.*

---

key /**kee**/ *noun* **keys**

1 an instrument for opening locks, winding clocks, etc
I tried to turn the key in the lock.

2 one of the levers or buttons struck by the fingers on a piano, computer, etc.
She ran her fingers down the piano keys.

3 something that when known enables you to work out a code, problem, etc.
They discovered the key to the puzzle.

→ *word family*
keyboard /**kee**-board/ *noun*
the set of levers or buttons struck by the fingers on a piano, computer, etc
I spilled water on the keyboard of the computer.

kick /kick/

* *verb* **kicks, kicking, kicked**
1 If you kick something, you strike it with your foot.
She kicked the ball into the net.

* *noun* **kicks**
1 a strike given with the foot
His leg was injured by a kick from a horse.
2 a thrill, a feeling of pleasure
He got a kick from driving fast cars.

kind¹ /kined/ *noun* **kinds**
1 sort, type, variety
There are various kinds of fruit available for breakfast.
2 character
The chocolates differ in size but not in kind.

→ *phrase*
If you **pay** for something **in kind**, you pay by goods, etc, not money.

kind² /kined/ *adjective* **kinder, kindest**
thoughtful and friendly, generous
Our kind neighbours made us dinner when our cooker broke down.

→ *word family*
kindness /kinde-ness/ *noun*
the quality of being kind
Their kindness was very touching.

kiss /kiss/

* *verb* **kisses, kissing, kissed**
to touch with the lips as a sign of love or respect
The children kissed their parents goodnight.

✳ *noun* **kisses**
a touch with the lips as a sign of love or respect
She gave him a kiss on the cheek.

knee /nee/ *noun* **knees**
the joint between the upper and lower parts of the leg

→ *word family*
kneel /neel/ *verb* **kneels**, **kneeling**, **knelt** /nelt/ or **kneeled** /neeld/
If you kneel, you go down or rest on the knees.
I knelt down to dig the weeds.

knife /nife/ *noun* **knives** /nivez/
a tool with a sharp edge for cutting
He was stabbed with a knife.
She carved the meat with a knife.

knit /nit/ *verb* **knits**, **knitting** /ni-ting/, **knitted** /ni-teed/
1 If you knit, you make woollen thread into garments by means of needles.
I knitted my husband a cardigan.
2 If two things knit together, they join together closely.
The broken bones failed to knit.

knot /not/
✳ *noun* **knots**
1 the twisting of two parts or pieces of string, etc, together so that they will not part until untied
She tied a knot in the string to keep the parcel together.

2 a hard piece of the wood of a tree, from which a branch grew out
There were several knots in the wood.

3 a small group of people
There was a knot of people gossiping at the corner.

* *verb* **knots, knotting, knotted**
If you knot something, you tie it in a knot.

know /no/ *verb* **knows, knowing, knew** /nyoo/, **known** /noan/

1 If you know something, you are aware of it.
She knew that he was there.

2 If you know about something, you have information about it.
She knows the office system thoroughly.
She did not know all the facts before she commented.

3 If you know a poem or a song, you have learned and remembered it.
Do you know that poem by Keats?

4 If you know someone, you are aware of their identity, and are acquainted with them.
I know Mary Jones.

➜ *word family*
knowing /no-wing/ *adjective*
showing secret understanding
a knowing smile
knowledge /nol-idge/ *noun*

1 those things that are known, information
He had considerable knowledge about America.

2 the whole of what can be learned or found out
There are many branches of knowledge in science.

knowledgeable /**nol**-idge-a-bil/ *adjective*
possessing knowledge or intelligence
She was very knowledgeable about politics.

label /**lay**-bel/

* *noun* **labels**
  a piece of paper or card fixed to something to give information about it
  Read the ingredients on the label.

* *verb* **labels, labelling** /**lay**-bu-ling/, **labelled** /**lay**-beld/
  If you label something, you fix a label to it.
  Please make sure all the parcels are labelled.

labour /**lay**-bur/

* *noun* **labours**

1 hard work
  The work was difficult manual labour.

2 childbirth
  She was in labour for several hours.

* *verb* **labours, labouring, laboured**

1 If you labour, you work hard.
  The men were labouring in the fields.

2 If you labour at something, you do it slowly or with difficulty.
  I have been labouring at this essay for weeks.

land /**land**/

* *noun* **lands**

1 the solid part of the Earth's surface
  I prefer being on land to the sea.

2 a country
  I would like to visit other lands.

3 ground, soil
The farmer's land is very fertile.

✳ *verb* **lands, landing, landed**

1 If you land something, you bring or put it down.
It was a female pilot who landed the plane.

2 If you land, or something lands, you reach the earth (for example, from air or from sea).
The plane landed safely.
We will land the cargo at Dover at midnight.

3 If you land a fish you catch it.
The angler landed a huge freshwater trout.

➔ *word family*
landing /**lan**-ding/ *noun*

1 the act of bringing something to earth
We had a bumpy landing.

2 a place for going on shore from water
Tie the boat up at the landing.

3 the corridor opening onto the rooms at the top of a flight of stairs
Go to the landing and you'll see my room straight ahead.

language /**lang**-gwidge/ *noun* **languages**

1 meaningful speech
Humans, unlike animals, use language.

2 the speech of a country or a people
She is fluent in the French language.

3 words
He was using obscene language.

large /**large**/ *adjective* **larger, largest**

more than usual in size, number, or amount
large sums of money
a large house

last¹ /**last**/ adjective

1 coming after all the others
He was last in the race.

2 latest
When was the last time you saw him?

3 final
This is the last episode in the series.

➔ *phrase*
If something is done **at last,** it is done in the end, finally.

last² /**last**/ verb **lasts, lasting, lasted**

If something lasts, it goes on.
The concert lasted until nine.

➔ *word family*
lasting /**la**-sting/ adjective
going on for a long time
a lasting reminder

late /**late**/

✳ adjective **later, latest**

1 far on in time
We were due to arrive in the late afternoon.

2 now dead
The flowers reminded the woman of her late husband.

3 recent
Have you heard the latest news on the crash?

✳ adverb

1 arriving after the time agreed
I was running late for the meeting.

2 at an advanced or old age
He became a successful writer late in life.

→ **word family**
lateness /**late**-ness/ *noun*
the state of being late

laugh /laf/

* *verb* **laughs, laughing, laughed**
to make a sound expressing amusement
I always laugh at his jokes.

* *noun* **laughs**
the sound of laughing
She heard a loud laugh coming from the other room.

→ **word family**
laughable /**la**-fa-bul/ *adjective*
causing people to laugh, ridiculous
his laughable attempts to jump the wall
laughter /**laf**-ter/ *noun*
the act or sound of laughing
the children's laughter

law /law/ *noun* **laws**

1 a rule or set of rules laid down for a group of
people by a recognized authority
These are the laws of the land.

2 in science, a statement of the way in which
objects regularly behave
the laws of physics

lay /lay/ *verb* **lays, laying, laid** /lade/

1 If you lay something or someone, you cause it or
them to lie.
He tried to lay the injured woman on the ground.

2 If you lay something on somewhere, you place it
there.
He laid the books on the table.

3 If you lay a table, you make it ready for a meal.
I laid the table for breakfast.

4 If a bird lays eggs, it produces them.
My hens lay eggs every day.

→ *phrase*
If you **lay yourself open to** something, you put yourself into the position of receiving it.

→ *usage*
Remember that the difference between **lay** and **lie** is that you **lay something down** and you **lie down**.

---

lead¹ /led/ *noun* **leads**

1 a soft heavy metal
The pipes in the house are made of lead.

2 the part of a pencil (actually made of graphite) used to write
The lead in my pencil broke.

---

lead² /leed/

∗ *verb* **leads, leading, led** /led/

1 If you lead the way, you go in front in order to guide.
He led the mountaineers up the cliff face.

2 If you lead a group of people, you act as a chief or commander.
The general was leading the attacking troops.

3 If you lead someone to do or think something, you influence them to do or think that.
She is very easily led by her friends.

4 If you lead your life a certain way, you spend it that way.
He leads a quiet life.

* *noun* **leads**

1 a guiding suggestion or example
Follow their lead.

2 the chief part in a play, film, or television programme
She has the lead in a local production of Saint Joan.

3 the position ahead of all others
She is in the lead in the race.

4 a cord, etc, for leading a dog
I put the dog on a lead before we go for a walk.

➔ *word family*
leader /**lee**-der/ *noun*

1 someone who shows the way
She's a born leader.

2 someone who gives orders or takes charge
the leader of the attacking force

3 a person or thing ahead of all the others
the leader in the competition
leadership /**lee**-der-ship/ *noun*
the act of being a leader
leading /**lee**-ding/ *adjective*
chief, most important
leading politicians

leaf /**leef**/ *noun* **leaves**

1 one of the thin, flat, usually green blades growing out of the stem of a plant or the branch of a tree
The leaves change colour in autumn.

2 a single sheet of paper in a book with pages printed on both sides
Turn over the leaves of the book.

→ idiom

If you **turn over a new leaf**, you begin to live or act in a better way.

lean¹ /leen/ *verb* **leans, leaning, leaned** /leend/ or **leant** /lent/

1   If something leans, it slopes to one side.
    The building leans to the right.

2   If you lean down to do something, you bend.
    She leaned down to pat the dog.

3   If you lean on or against something, you rest against it.
    The ladder was leaning against the wall.

4   If you lean towards something, you have a preference for it.
    We are now leaning towards a June wedding.

lean² /leen/ *adjective* **leaner, leanest**

slim, thin, containing very little fat
I use lean beef in my chilli con carne.

leap /leep/

✳   *verb* **leaps, leaping, leaped** /leept/ or **leapt** /lept/
    If you leap, you jump.
    He leapt out of bed on Christmas morning.
    We saw a deer leaping over the fence.

✳   *noun* **leaps**
    a jump
    The horse cleared the fence in one leap.

learn /lern/ *verb* **learns, learning, learned** /lernd/ or **learnt** /lernt/

1   If you learn something, you gain knowledge of it or the skills necessary to do it.
    I have been learning French.
    The children have learned how to swim.

2 If you learn a lesson, you come to understand or realize something.

She must learn that she has to consider others.

3 If you learn a poem or song, you fix it in your memory.

I learned a poem by Keats for my homework.

→ *word family*

learned /**ler**-ned/ *adjective*

having a lot of knowledge, gained by study

He's a very learned old gentleman.

learner /**ler**-ner/ *noun*

someone who is learning something

The driver of the car in front is a learner.

learners of English as a foreign language

learning /**ler**-ning/ *noun*

knowledge gained by study

a man of learning

leave /**leev**/

---

* *noun*

1 permission

She received leave to go home early.

2 permitted absence

She is on sick leave.

3 holiday

I will be on annual leave for most of July.

4 farewell

He took his leave from them.

* *verb* **leaves, leaving, left** /**left**/

1 If you leave something in a particular state or condition, you cause it to be or remain that way.

I asked him to leave the door open.

The resignation has left the country without a leader.

2   If you leave somewhere, you depart.
    He left home at an early age.

3   If you leave something somewhere, you go away
    without taking it with you.
    She left her gloves in the car.

4   If you leave someone with whom you are in a
    relationship, you go away and stop living with them.
    He has left his wife.

5   If you leave something behind, you allow it to
    remain unused, untaken, uneaten, etc
    She left most of the meal.

---

left /left/ *noun*

When you look at the word *it*, the letter *i* is on the
left, the side opposite to the right.
In this country we drive on the left of the road.

→   *word family*
    left-handed /left–han-did/ *adjective*
    better able to use the left hand than the right
    left-handed people

---

leg /leg/ *noun* **legs**

1   one of the limbs on which a person or animal
    stands or moves
    I broke my leg falling off the wall.

2   a support for a table, chair, etc
    The kitchen table has uneven legs.

3   a stage of a competition or tournament
    This is the last leg of the race.

→   *idioms*
    If you are **on your last legs,** you are near the end of
    your power, life, etc.
    If you **pull a person's leg,** you play a joke on them.

lend /lend/ *verb* **lends, lending, lent** /lent/

If you lend someone something, you give it to them on condition that they give it back to you at a later time.

Don't lend him any money.

→ *word family*

lender /len-der/ *noun*

someone who lends something to someone

length /lenth/ *noun* **lengths**

the measurement of something from end to end of space or time

Could you estimate the length of the journey?

→ *phrase*

at length

1 at last

At length we understood what he was trying to say.

2 taking a long time, in detail

She explained the plan at length.

→ *word family*

lengthen /lenth-en/ *verb*

to make or become longer

I will have to lengthen the bedroom curtains.

lengthy /lenth-ee/ *adjective*

very long

a lengthy sermon

a lengthy delay

less /less/

* *adjective* **lesser, least**

smaller, not so much

He's going to earn less money in his new job.

✷ *noun*
a smaller amount
He had already eaten sweets that day, so when it came time for pudding she gave him less.

✷ *adverb*
not so greatly, not so much
She likes him less now she knows he lied.

→ *word family*
lessen /**le**-sun/ *verb*
If you lessen something, you make it become less.
This will lessen the pain.
lesser /**le**-ser/ *adjective*
less, smaller
a lesser problem

→ *usage*
Remember that less is used with uncountable nouns, for example: **less time**. If you are talking about countable nouns in the plural, you use fewer: **fewer hours**.

let /let/

✷ *verb* **lets, letting** /**le**-ting/, **let** /let/
1 If you let someone do something, you allow them to do it.
She let her children go to the cinema.
I let him talk me into buying the car.
2 If you let a house or flat, you allow it to be used for rent or payment.
They let a room in their house to a student.

✷ *noun* **lets**
the act of letting a room or property for rent
This is a short-term let.

letter /**le**-ter/ *noun* **letters**

1 a sign standing for a sound
   the letter h
2 a written message
   He was asked to write a letter of apology.
➔ *phrases*
   A **letter of credit** is one allowing the holder to
   draw money when away from home.
   If something is done **to the letter**, it is done
   exactly as it should be.

level /**le**-vel/

∗ *noun* **levels**
1 a flat, even surface
   He can walk on the level but not uphill.
2 a general standard of quality or quantity
   He has met a high level of achievement.
3 a horizontal division or floor in a house, etc
   Their garden is on two levels.
∗ *adjective*
1 flat
   They walked across the level floor.
2 even
   Are the two sides level?
∗ *verb* **levels**, **levelling** /**le**-ve-ling/, **levelled** /**le**-veld/
1 If you level ground, you make it flat.
   He used a digger to level the ground.
2 If you level a game, you make the scores equal.
   The team would like to level the score.

library /**lie**-bre-ree/ *noun* **libraries**

1 a collection of books
   The building holds a fiction library and a reference library.

2   a room or building in which books are kept
Plans to build a new library have been cancelled.

---

lie¹ /lie/

∗ *noun* **lies**
   a statement that the maker knows to be untrue
   He told a lie to try to avoid being punished.

∗ *verb* **lies, lying** /lie-ing/, **lied** /lied/
   If you lie, you say something that is untrue.
   It was obvious that he was lying.

---

lie² /lie/ *verb* **lay** /lay/, **lying** /lie-ing/, **lain** /lane/

---

1   If you lie on something, you put your body full
   length upon it.
   She wants to lie on the beach all day.

2   If something lies somewhere, it sits or remains in
   a certain place.
   The book was lying on the table.

---

lift /lift/

∗ *verb* **lifts, lifting, lifted**

1   If you lift something, you raise it up so it is
   higher than it was.
   He lifted the flag above his head.

2   If you lift someone, you take them up in your
   arms.
   I lifted the baby from the pram.

∗ *noun* **lifts**

1   a machine by which people or goods are carried
   from floor to floor in a building
   We took the lift up to the 15th floor.

2   a free ride in a private vehicle
   I get a lift to work from my neighbour.

light¹ /lite/

∗ *noun* **lights**

1 that which makes it possible for the eye to see things

   I could see clearly in the light.

2 anything that gives light, such as the sun, a lamp, etc

   I turned on the bedside light to read my book.

3 knowledge, understanding

   I am unable to throw any light on the problem.

4 brightness in the eyes or face

   There was a twinkly light in his eye.

∗ *adjective* **lighter, lightest**

1 clear, not dark

   It's getting light.

2 not deep or dark in colour

   He was wearing a light green shirt.

   She had light blonde hair.

∗ *verb* **lights, lighting, lit** /lit/

   If you light something, you give light to it or set fire to it.

   He lit the fire.

light² /lite/ *adjective* **lighter, lightest**

1 not heavy

   Only light loads are allowed on this bridge.

2 not difficult

   She can do light tasks at the moment as she is inexperienced.

3 not severe

   He was given a light punishment for the crime.

4 small in amount

   March saw very light rainfall.

5 not serious, for entertainment
I'd like some light reading as I'm quite tired.
6 graceful
She's very light on her feet when she dances.
7 happy, merry
He's so cheerful and light of heart.

like¹ /like/

* *adjective*
nearly the same, resembling
We have like attitudes to work.
They are very like each other.
* *preposition*
in the same way as
She walks like her mother.
* *noun* **likes**
a person or thing nearly the same as or equal to another
You will never see his like again.

like² /like/ *verb* **likes, liking, liked**

1 If you like something, you are pleased by it.
She liked the play.
2 If you like someone, you are fond of them.
She really likes her next-door neighbour.
→ *word family*
likeable, likable /like-a-bul/ *adjective*
attractive, pleasant

limit /li-mit/

* *noun* **limits**
1 a boundary
They drove outside the city limits.

2 that which you may not go past
The children were testing the limits of his patience.

3 the greatest or smallest amount or number that is fixed as being correct, legal, necessary, desirable, etc
The company imposed a four per cent limit on pay increases.

✱ *verb* **limits, limiting, limited**
If you limit something, you keep it within set boundaries.
Try to limit your expenditure on entertainment.

➜ *word family*
limitation /li-mi-**tay**-shun/ *noun*

1 that which limits
time limitations

2 inability to do something, weakness
All of us have our limitations.
limited /**li**-mi-ted/ *adjective*

1 small in amount
a limited supply of food

2 not very great, large, wide-ranging, etc
of limited experience

---

lip /lip/ *noun* **lips**

1 either of the edges of the opening of the mouth
She bit her lip to try to stop crying.

2 the edge or brim of anything
The lip of the cup had a small chip in it.

➜ *word family*
lip-read /**lip**-reed/ *verb*
If you lip-read, you understand what a person is saying from the movements of his or her lips.
She is deaf and she lip-reads well.

liquid /**li**-kwid/

∗ *noun* **liquids**

a substance that is not solid and can be poured.

Water is a liquid.

∗ *adjective*

in the form of a liquid

They have liquid soap in the bathroom.

list /list/

∗ *noun* **lists**

a series of names, numbers, etc, written down in order one after the other

I'm writing a shopping list.

There is a long list of people waiting for houses.

∗ *verb* **lists, listing, listed**

If you list something, you write it down or speak it in some sort of order.

I asked him to list all the people present at the party.

➔ *usage*

You write something **on** a list, not **in** a list.

listen /**li**-sen/ *verb* **listens, listening, listened**

1 If you listen to something, you try to hear it.

She likes to listen to music as she works.

2 If you listen to someone, you pay attention to them.

He decided to listen to his mother's advice.

➔ *word family*

listener /**li**-sner/ *noun*

someone who listens

My doctor is a very good listener.

little /**li**-tul/

* *adjective* **littler, littlest**

1 small

There were two little birds in the garden.

2 short

He is the littlest of all the boys in the class.

3 young

There are lots of little children here.

* *noun*

a small amount

They pay a little at a time.

* *adverb*

not much, not highly

They think little of her work.

live¹ /**liv**/ *verb* **lives, living, lived**

1 If you live, you have life and exist.
We all have the right to live.

2 If you live, you continue to be alive.
He is very ill but he will live.

3 If you live in a place, that is the place where you have your home.
She lives in the country.

4 If you live in a certain way, you behave in that certain way.
live dangerously

➔ *phrase*

If you **live** something **down**, you behave in a way that makes others overlook your past faults.

live² /**live**/ *adjective*

1 having life, alive
a cat with a live mouse

2   full of energy, capable of becoming active
  live electrical wires

3   heard or seen as the event takes place, not
  recorded
  a live broadcast

4   burning
  live coals

➔   ***word family***
  living /**li**-ving/ *noun*
  a means of providing oneself with what is
  necessary for life
  What does he do for a living?

lock /lok/

✳   *noun* **locks**

1   a fastening bolt moved by a key
  I turned the key in the lock.

2   a section of a canal, enclosed by gates, in
  which the amount of water can be increased or
  decreased to raise or lower a boat
  The boat waited at the lock for several hours.

3   a curl of hair
  She cut a lock of her hair.

✳   *verb* **locks, locking, locked**

1   If you lock a door, you fasten it with a lock and
  key.
  I locked the door before I went to bed.

2   If something locks, it becomes fixed or blocked.
  The car's wheels have locked.

➔   ***idiom***
  If you do something **lock, stock, and barrel,** you do
  it completely.

long /lawng/

✽ adjective **longer, longest**

1 not short in time or space
It was a long journey home.
a long road

2 having length, covering a certain distance from one end to the other or a certain time
The garden was very long.
The film was two hours long.

✽ verb **longs, longing, longed**
If you long for something, you want it very much.
She longs to see her friend again.

lose /looz/ verb **loses, losing, lost** /lost/

1 If you lose something, you cease to have it.
He lost his eye in an accident.

2 If you lose an object, you fail to keep it.
She lost her gloves.

3 If you lose a game or a battle, you are defeated.
They lost the battle.

4 If you lose time, you waste it.
He lost no time in asking for a loan.

5 If you lose an opportunity, you miss it.
They lost the opportunity to buy the house.

➔ *idiom*
If you **lose your head**, you become too excited to act sensibly.

loss /loss/ noun **losses**

1 the act of losing
His team had nine losses during the football season.
He couldn't get over the loss of his wife.

2 something which has been lost
His departure is a loss to the firm.

3 harm, damage
He was forced to pay for the losses.

➔ *idiom*
If you are **at a loss**, you do not know what to do.

---

loud /**loud**/ *adjective* **louder, loudest**

1 easily heard
He has a very loud voice.

2 noisy
It was a loud party.

3 unpleasantly bright, showy
She wore loud colours.

---

love /**luv**/

✳ *noun* **loves**

1 a strong liking for
He has a love of good food.

2 a strong feeling or desire for
He is full of love for his wife.

3 the person or thing loved
His first love is opera.

✳ *verb* **loves**, **loving**, **loved**

1 If you love something, you like it very much.
He loves Mexican food.

2 If you love someone, you are strongly attracted to them.
He loved her and was heartbroken when she left.

➔ *word family*
lover /**lu**-ver/ *noun*
a person who loves someone or something
He's a real book lover.

low /lo/ *adjective* **lower, lowest**

1 not far above the ground
   The picture is too low.

2 not tall, not high
   The buildings are very low.

3 small in degree, amount, etc
   The temperature was very low.

4 not high in rank or position
   He had a low position in the firm.

5 cheap
   The prices there are really low.

6 soft, not loud
   He has a low voice.

7 sad, unhappy
   He is feeling really low just now.

➔ *idiom*
   If you are **in low spirits**, you are in a sad mood.

lower /lo-er/ *verb* **lowers, lowering, lowered**

1 If you lower something, you make it less high.
   We decided to lower the height of the ceiling.

2 If something is lowered down, it is let or brought
   down.
   The flag was lowered.

3 If the value or worth of something is lowered, it is
   made less valuable.
   *The building of the motorway lowered the value of
   their property.*

luck /luck/ *noun*

1 the good or bad things that happen by chance,
   fate, fortune, etc
   Only luck is involved, not skill.

She has had bad luck with boyfriends.

2 something good that happens by chance
Luck was with her.

➔ *word family*

luckless /**luck**-less/ *adjective*
unfortunate
He was a luckless loser.

lucky /**lu**-kee/ *adjective*
fortunate, having good luck
She is very lucky and is always winning things.
It is lucky that you spotted that parking space.

---

machine /ma-**sheen**/ *noun* **machines**

1 any apparatus for producing power or doing work

➔ *collocation*
I **put on** the **washing machine**.

2 a system or organization that works well
He was the man behind the political party's machine.

---

main /**mane**/

✱ *adjective*
chief, principal
The company's main office is in New York.

➔ *collocation*
*The rent from the property is his **main source** of income.*

✱ *noun* **mains**

1 the greater part of something

2 (**mains**) a pipe underground for water, gas, etc

major /**may**-jor/

* *adjective*

1 the greater in number, size, or quantity
   the major part of the audience

2 the more important
   These scientists have made major medical discoveries.

* *noun* **majors**
   an army officer just above a captain in rank

→ *word family*
   majority /ma-**jaw**-ri-tee/ *noun*

1 the greater number
   The teacher is liked by the majority of the class.

2 in voting, the amount by which the number of votes cast for one candidate exceeds that cast for another
   The government won by a majority of thousands.

make /**make**/

* *verb* **makes, making, made** /**made**/

1 If you make something, you create or construct it.
   Today the children made cakes.
   I made a model aeroplane out of a kit.

2 If someone or something makes someone something, it causes them to be that thing.
   The win made him famous.

3 If someone makes someone else do something, they force them to do it.
   They made her climb the hill.

4 If you make a certain amount of money, you earn it.
   He makes around £40 thousand a year.

✳ *noun* **makes**

the company that makes something, or the method by which it is made

What make are your trainers?

➔ *phrases*

If you **make for something**, you go towards it.

If you **make good**, you succeed or do well.

If you **make off**, you run away.

If you **make something out**, you decipher it.

If you **make up** a story, you invent it.

If you **make up** your face, you put cosmetics on it.

If you **make up** after a fight or quarrel, you put an end to it.

➔ *word family*

make-believe /**make**-bi-leev/ *noun*

the act of pretending

It was just make-believe that she was a princess.

make-over /**make**-oe-ver/ *noun*

the process of trying to improve the appearance of a person or place

maker /**make**-er/ *noun*

a person who makes something

a maker of furniture

---

male /**male**/ *adjective*

of or relating to the sex that can become a father

a male elephant

---

man /**man**/

✳ *noun* **men** /**men**/

1 the human race

Man has destroyed much of the environment.

2 a human being
All men must die.

3 a male human being
the man over there

4 a husband
Her man was out for the evening.

* *verb* **mans, manning, manned**
If you man something, you provide it with
sufficient workers to make it work.
We need to man the lifeboats.

---

many /**men**-ee/

* *adjective*
great in number
Many people would like to live in the area.

* *noun*
a large number
Many of my friends have dogs.

➔ *usage*
Remember that **many** is only used with countable
nouns, and **much** is used with uncountable nouns.

---

market /**mar**-ket/

* *noun* **markets**

1 a public place for buying and selling
*I always buy my vegetables at the weekly farmers'
market.*

2 a demand or need
There's a market for lightweight cotton clothing.

* *verb* **markets, marketing, marketed**
If you market something, you sell it.
They market their books all over the world.

match

→ *word family*
marketable /**mar**-ke-ta-bul/ *adjective*
used to describe something that can be sold
These products are no longer easily marketable.
marketing /**mar**-ke-ting/ *noun*
the promoting and selling of a product

match¹ /**match**/ *noun* **matches**

a small stick tipped with a substance that catches fire when rubbed on certain prepared surfaces
I lit the fire with a match.

match² /**match**/

* *noun* **matches**
1 a person or thing that is the same or nearly the same as another
I would like to find a match for the wool.
2 an equal
She was his match in any argument.
3 a sporting contest or game
a football match
4 a marriage or relationship
They make a great match.
* *verb* **matches, matching, matched**
1 If something matches something else, it is equal to it.
The city restaurant does not match our local one for home cooking.
2 If one thing matches another, it is like it or it goes well with it.
The dress matches her eyes.

material /ma-**teer**-ee-al/

* *adjective*

1   to do with money or belongings rather than anything spiritual
    She has material interests.

2   important, relevant

➔   *usage*

    In quite formal usage, you say something is **material to** something if it is relevant. If something is not important or not relevant, you say it is **immaterial**. This is more common to hear.
    It's immaterial whether the man is guilty or not, by law he's entitled to a fair trial.

* *noun* **materials**

1   the substance out of which a thing is made
    I use only good-quality materials in my buildings.

2   the subject matter, facts, or content of something
    The comedian had some hilarious material.
    He has some wild stories – great material for a book.

3   cloth
    My coat is made of a warm material.

➔   *word family*

    materialistic /ma-**teer**-ee-al-is-tik/ *adjective*
    concerned with money and material wealth
    She's very materialistic and is always talking about the expensive gifts her husband has been buying her.

matter /**ma**-ter/

* *noun* **matters**

1   a subject
    an interesting matter for discussion

→ **collocation**
What is **the matter**?

2 an affair
This is a family matter.

3 a substance or type of thing
The compost is made up of vegetable matter.

✳ *verb* **matters, mattering, mattered**
If something matters, it is of importance.
It doesn't matter if you can't be there.
It matters to me that you made an effort to be here today.

→ **word family**
matter-of-fact /ma-ter-ov-**fact**/ *adjective*
without exaggeration, or concerning facts only
It was a matter-of-fact description of the situation.

---

me /**mee**/ *pronoun*

the form of the pronoun I used when it is the object of a sentence
I know you but you don't know me.

→ **word family**
mine /**mine**/ *pronoun*
belonging to the speaker or writer
This coat is mine and this one is yours.
myself /**mie**-self/ *reflexive pronoun* of I or **me**
referring to the speaker
I want to sort out this mess by myself.
I'm not feeling like myself today.
my /**mie**/ *determiner*
belonging to the speaker or writer
It is my right to see the child.

→ *usage*

Remember that **me** is used after a verb or preposition, not before a verb.

---

mean¹ /meen/ *adjective* **meaner, meanest**

1 nasty, unkind over small things
   She's really mean to her younger sister.

2 unwilling to spend money
   My brother is too mean to give presents.

→ *word family*

meanness /meen-ness/ *noun*
the quality of being mean

---

mean² /meen/ *verb* **means, meaning, meant** /ment/

1 If you mean to do something, you intend to do it.
   We did not mean to hurt her.

2 If something is meant to be a certain thing, it has a certain purpose.
   This carpet was meant for the sitting room.

3 If you mean something, you try to express a certain idea.
   She did not know what the word meant.

---

mean³ /meen/

∗ *adjective*

1 middle
   the mean point

2 halfway between numbers, amounts, extremes, etc
   the mean annual rainfall

∗ *noun* **means**

1 the average
   the mean of the quantities

2 a middle state
   the mean between being too harsh and being too kind

medical /**me**-di-cal/ *adjective*

having to do with medicine, the work of a doctor, or healing

She is on the medical staff at the hospital.

→ *word family*

medically /**me**-di-ca-lee/ *adverb*

done in a medical way

She was treated medically.

meet /**meet**/ *verb* **meets, meeting, met** /**met**/

1 If you meet someone, you come face to face with them, often by chance.
   I met my neighbour on the street.
2 If two people meet, they come together by arrangement.
   We meet for lunch once a week.
3 If you meet a payment, you make the payment.
   He is unable to meet his debts.
4 If you meet the requirements of something, you satisfy those requirements.
   They could not meet the demands of the kidnappers.

→ *word family*

meeting /**mee**-ting/ *noun*

a coming together for a special purpose

There was a meeting of parents and teachers at the school.

→ *collocation*

*There was a **committee meeting** on Tuesday night.*
*I have a **business meeting** in the morning.*

member /**mem**-ber/ *noun* **members**

one of a society or group

→ **collocation**
He became a member of the chess club.

memory /**me**-mu-ree/ *noun* **memories**
1 the power of the mind to recall past events or to learn things by heart
→ **collocation**
I have a poor memory.
2 the mind's store of remembered things
My sister's memory is full of useful facts.
3 something remembered
The book brought back childhood memories.
4 the part of a computer that stores information
I had to buy extra memory for my computer.
→ **word family**
memorize /**me**-mu-rize/ *verb* **memorizes, memorizing, memorized**
If you memorize something, you learn it so that you can say it without having to read it.
I tried to memorize the telephone number.

method /**me**-thod/ *noun* **methods**
1 a way of doing something
He did not like their method of doing business.
2 an orderly way of arranging or doing things
Their office system is lacking method.

middle /**mi**-dul/
✳ *adjective*
equally distant from the ends or limits
I sat on the middle seat in the row.
✳ *noun* **middles**
the centre of something, the middle part or point
I was standing in the middle of the circle.

might /**mite**/ *noun*

> power, strength
> *The army was crushed by the might of the enemy.*

mind /**minde**/

✱ *noun* **minds**
1 the power by which human beings understand, think, feel, etc
   She has a sharp mind.
   Her mind was on other things.
2 a person of great mental ability
   one of the great minds of our time
3 memory
   I was unable to call his name to mind.

✱ *verb* **minds**, **minding**, **minded**
1 If you mind someone or something, you take care of them or it.
   Could I ask you to mind the baby?
2 If you mind something in front of you, you take heed of it.
   Mind you don't fall on the ice!
3 If you mind about something, you object to it.
   I do not mind if you leave early.

➔ *idioms*
   If you **mind your Ps and Qs,** you are careful about what you say or do.
   If you **mind your own business,** you do not interfere in the affairs of other people.

➔ *word family*
   minded /**mine**-did/ *adjective*
   tending to be
   serious-minded

mindful /**minde**-ful/ *adjective*

not forgetful, paying attention to
always mindful of possible dangers

mindless /**minde**-less/ *adjective*

unthinking, stupid
a mindless act of violence

minute[1] /**mi**-nit/ *noun* **minutes**

* *noun* **minutes**
1 the 60th part of an hour
It took us 30 minutes to get home.
2 a short time
I'll be with you in a minute.
3 (**minutes**) a short account of what was discussed
and decided at a meeting
➔ *collocation*
*I was asked **to take the minutes** of the meeting.*
* *verb* **minutes, minuting, minuted**
If you minute something, you make a written
note of it.
I minuted our discussion.

minute[2] /mie-**nyoot**/ *adjective*
1 very small
Minute quantities of the drug were found.
2 exact
She pays minute attention to detail.

model /**mo**-del/

* *noun* **models**
1 a person or thing to be copied
I tried to use the essay as a model.

2 a copy, usually smaller, of a person or thing
He made models of aircraft.

3 a living person who sits or stands still to let an artist draw him or her
He was chosen as a model for the art class.

4 a person who is employed to display clothes by wearing them
The models were on their way to Paris fashion week.

5 an artificial figure used in display
shop-window models

✳ *adjective*
worth copying, perfect

➜ *collocation*
*The child displayed **model behaviour**.*

✳ *verb* **models, modelling, modelled**

1 If you model something, you give shape to it.
He modelled the clay into a bowl.

2 If you model clothes, you wear them to show to possible buyers
She was modelling the new season's fashions.

➜ *phrase*
If something is **modelled on** something, it is an intentional imitation or copy.
*Her style is **modelled on** that of Audrey Hepburn.*
*She **models herself on** Audrey Hepburn.*

modern /**mod**-ern/ *adjective*

1 belonging to the present day
This is a very modern book.

2 belonging to recent centuries
She studies modern history.

3 up-to-date
My parents have modern ideas on education.

→ *word family*
modernity /mo-**der**-ni-tee/ *noun*
the state of being modern
modernize /**mod**-er-nize/ *verb* **modernizes,
modernizing, modernized**
If you modernize something, you bring it up to date.
*The company are modernizing machinery to keep
ahead of the competition.*

moment /**mo**-ment/ *noun* **moments**
a very short time
It took only a moment to get on the boat.

money /**mu**-nee/ *noun*
metal coins and printed banknotes used in
making payments, buying, and selling

month /**munth**/ *noun* **months**
one of the twelve periods of time into which the
year is divided
I went to the outside swimming pool last month.

morning /**mawr**-ning/ *noun* **mornings**
the early part of the day, before noon
I go to work at eight in the morning.

mother /**mu**-ther/
✻ *noun* **mothers**
1 a female parent
I asked my mother to help me with the children.
2 the female head of a convent of nuns
✻ *verb* **mothers, mothering, mothered**
If you mother someone, you care for them in the
way that a mother would.
She mothered the orphans.

mouth

→ **thesaurus**
ma, mamma, maw, mom, mommy, mum, mummy
→ **word family**
grandmother *also* **grandma, gran, granny, nan, nanna, nana** *noun*
your father's mother, your mother's mother

---

mouth /**mouth**/

* *noun* **mouths**

1 the opening in the face for eating and uttering sounds
She opened her mouth to scream.

2 the opening into anything hollow
The jam spilled over the mouth of the jar.

3 the part of a river where it flows into the sea

* *verb* **mouths, mouthing, mouthed**
If you mouth something, you silently make words with your mouth.
She mouthed the answer to him across the classroom.

---

move /**moov**/

* *verb* **moves, moving, moved**

1 If you move something somewhere, you cause it to change place or position.
I wanted to move the chairs to the next room.

2 If you move to a place, you go there from another place.
I have moved house three times in the last decade.

3 If you move to do something, you start to set it in motion.

4 If you are moved by something, your feelings are stirred by it.
I was terribly moved by the film.

5 If you move someone to action, you rouse them to it.

She moved them to protest.

* *noun* **moves**

1 a change of position or place

The house move was exhausting.

2 an action

I wonder what his next move will be.

→ *word family*

movement /**moov**-ment/ *noun*

1 act of moving

The police are watching his movements.

2 change of position

The sudden movement made the dog bark.

3 a number of people working for the same purpose

the women's movement

4 a complete part of a long musical work

I love the slow movement of this piece of music.

moveable /**moo**-va-bul/ *adjective*

able to be moved

The table is moveable.

moving /**moo**-ving/ *adjective*

causing your feelings to be stirred

It was a very moving performance.

Mr /**miss**-ter/ *noun*

a title used before a man's name, especially in the address on an envelope

Mrs /**mi**-siz/ *noun*

a title used before a married woman's name

→ **word family**
Miss /miss/ *noun*
a title used before an unmarried woman's name
Ms /miz/ *noun*
a title used before a woman's name, which
doesn't indicate whether she is married or not

much /**much**/

* *adjective*
  great in amount or quantity
  He doesn't have much money.
* *noun*
  a great amount
  He does not earn much.
* *adverb*
  greatly
  He was much moved by the film.
→ **usage**
  Remember that **much** is only used with
  uncountable nouns, and **many** is used with
  countable nouns.

music /**myoo**-zic/ *noun*

1 the art of arranging sounds to give melody or
   harmony
   My sister is studying music.
2 the sounds so arranged when played, sung, or
   written down
   I listen to orchestral music.
→ **usage**
   Music is always used as a singular noun.
→ **word family**
   musical /**myoo**-zi-cal/

* *adjective*
1   having to do with music
    My aunt enjoys musical theatre.
2   pleasant-sounding
    She has a very musical voice.
* *noun* **musicals**
    a play or film that includes a lot of songs
    musician /myoo-**zi**-shun/ *noun*
    a person who is skilled in music
    The musicians were late for rehearsal.

must /**must**/ *verb*

If you must do something, you have to do it.
I must go home now.

name /**name**/

* *noun* **names**
1   the word by which a person or thing is known
→   *collocation*
    The ticket inspector **asked** *my* **name**.
2   reputation
    He has made a name for himself in the art world.
* *verb* **names, naming, named**
1   If you name someone, you give a name to them.
    They are naming the baby Alice.
2   If you name something, you say it by name.
    I can name all the country's presidents.
* *adjective*
    carrying a name
    a name tag
→   *word family*
    nameless /**name**-less/ *adjective*
1   unknown
    It was written by a nameless poet of the twelfth century.

2 having no name
The cemetery was filled with nameless graves.

3 wanting their name to be concealed
The giver of the money wishes to remain nameless.
namely /**name**-lee/ *adverb*
that is to say
Only one student was absent, namely Peter.

---

nature /**nay**-chur/

✱ *noun* **natures**

1 everything that exists and happens in the universe that is not the work of humans, such as plants, animals, mountains, lakes, etc

2 the sum of those qualities that make any creature or thing different from others
This is the nature of the new drug.

3 the character of a person
She has a sweet nature.

4 kind, sort

➔ *collocation*
*I need to know the **nature of** his injuries before I can treat him.*

➔ *word family*
natural /**na**-chur-al/ *adjective*

1 relating to or occurring in nature
I love using natural products on my skin.

2 not needing to be explained, innate, unlearned
It's natural to feel sad when a pet dies.

---

near /**neer**/

✱ *adjective* **nearer, nearest**

1 close, not distant in time or place
We didn't bother catching a taxi as the station was so near.

2 only just missed or avoided

➔ *collocation*
  That was *a near miss.*

✻ *preposition*
  close to
  Don't come near me.

✻ *adverb*
  almost
  The holidays are drawing near.

✻ *verb* **nears, nearing, neared**
  If you **near something,** you approach it.
  She neared the train station.

➔ *word family*
  nearby /**neer**-bie/ *adjective, adverb*
  near, close by
  She loved visiting the nearby shops.
  nearer /**nee**-rer/ *adverb, adjective, preposition*
  less distant from
  The planet is nearer the sun than Earth.
  nearest /**nee**-rest/ *adverb, adjective, preposition*
  least distant from
  Mercury is nearest to the sun.
  nearly /**neer**-lee/ *adverb*
  almost
  He nearly died.
  It's nearly time to go.

necessary /**ne**-si-se-ree/ *adjective*

  needed, unavoidable, that which cannot be done
  without
  *I need to take the necessary classes in order to get
  my degree.*

need

→ *word family*
necessarily /ne-si-**se**-ri-lee/ *adverb*
unavoidably

→ *collocation*
It's **not necessarily** the case.

need /**need**/

* *noun* **needs**
1 a want
   The dog is in need of food.
2 things which one requires
   We have few needs in this office.
3 poverty
   These families are living in need.

* *verb* **needs, needing, needed**
1 If you need something, you are in want of it.
   They need food and warm clothing.

→ *collocation*
I **need help** with the housework.
2 If you need to do something, you have to do it.
   The boys will need to work harder at school.

→ *word family*
needful /**need**-ful/ *adjective*
necessary
Take the needful steps to avoid infection.

new /**nyoo**/ *adjective* **newer, newest**
1 never known before
   He is full of new and exciting ideas.
2 just bought or made, fresh

→ *collocation*
I need **new clothes**.
I was hoping to get a **new car**.

3 changed from an earlier state, different
➔ *collocation*
I'd like a **new job.**
She's a **new mother.**
➔ *word family*
newness /**nyoo**-ness/ *noun*
the state of being new
newborn /**nyoo**-bawrn/ *noun*
a recently born infant
newcomer /**nyoo**-cu-mer/ *noun*
a person who has recently arrived at a place
The newcomers to the club were welcomed by the older members.
newly /**nyoo**-lee/ *adverb*
recently
We have newly laid eggs from the chickens.

next /**nekst**/ *adjective*
nearest, just before or just after in time, place, degree, or rank
They live in the next street.
We are going to Oxford on Thursday, then London the next day.
➔ *word family*
next door /**nekst**-door/ *adjective*
in or at the next house or building
the garden next door

nice /**nice**/ *adjective* **nicer, nicest**
pleasing, attractive, kind
➔ *collocation*
They had a really **nice day** at the park.
We had a **nice meal** at the restaurant.

→ *thesaurus*
pleasant, pleasing, kind, friendly

night /**nite**/ *noun* **nights** *Also* **night time** /**nite**-time/
the time between sunset and sunrise, darkness

→ *collocation*
*Lots of animals come out **at night.***

no /**noe**/

＊ *sentence substitute*
not ever, the opposite of **yes**, it cannot be so.
Would I ever go out with him? No.

＊ *determiner*
not any, not one, not at all
There's no bread left.
He's no fool.

＊ *noun*
an answer of no; not
Is he through to round two? It's a no from me.

→ *word family*
nobody /**noe**-buddy/, **no one** /**noe**-wun/ *pronoun*
no person, not anyone
Nobody loves me.
none /**nun**/ *pronoun*
not any
None of my children have gone to university.
nowhere /**noe**-ware/ *adverb*
not anywhere
My career is going nowhere.

normal /**nor**-mal/ *adjective*
usual, according to what is expected, average
His body temperature was higher than normal.

→ *collocation*
I'm not sure this is **normal behaviour**.
What is your husband's **normal routine?**

→ *word family*
normality /nor-**ma**-li-tee/ *noun*
the state of being normal

---

not /**not**/ *adverb*

in no manner, to no degree

---

note /**note**/

❋ *noun* **notes**
1 a short letter
I'd like to write them a note to thank them.
2 a short written account of what is said or done
She took notes at the committee meeting.
3 a written explanation
She scribbled a note at the foot of the page.
4 a single musical sound or the sign standing for it
❋ *verb* **notes**, **noting**, **noted**
If you note something, you put it down in writing.
The policeman noted the details of the accident.

→ *collocation*
He **noted down** her number.

→ *word family*
notebook /**note**-book/ *noun*
a book into which notes may be written
noted /**no**-tid/ *adjective*
famous, well known
a noted director
notepad /**note**-pad/ *noun*
a small pad of paper for writing on

notepaper /**note**-pay-per/ *noun*
paper for writing notes or letters on

nothing /**nu**-thing/ *noun*

1 no thing, not anything
There's absolutely nothing in the cupboard.
2 a thing of no importance
Her friendship is nothing to him.

now /**now**/ *noun*

1 at the present time
She lives in London now.
2 at once
Go now!

number /**num**-ber/

* *noun* **numbers**
1 a word or sign that tells how many
a phone number
2 a collection of several people, things, etc
a small number of viewers
* *verb* **numbers, numbering, numbered**
1 If something numbers an amount, it reaches that amount as a total.
The spectators numbered a thousand.
2 If someone is numbered among other people, they are included among them.

➔ *collocation*
*He is **numbered among** our greatest scientists.*

obvious /**ob**-vee-us/ *adjective*
easily seen or understood
There is a very obvious solution to the problem.

of /ov/ *preposition*

1 belonging to
   the shore of the lake
2 relating to
   a tale of the Wild West
3 made of
   a ring of gold
4 from
   south of the border

off /off/

∗ *adverb*
1 away
   They drove off from the house.
2 distant
   The shop was a few miles off.
∗ *adjective*
1 not happening
   The match is off.
2 not fit to eat, bad, rotten
   This meat is off.
∗ *preposition*
   away from, not on
   Take your foot off the table.
→ **collocation**
   Keep off *the grass.*

offer /**off**-er/

∗ *verb* **offers, offering, offered**
1 If you offer someone a chance, you give them the
   chance of taking it.
   I am thinking of offering him a job.
2 If you offer to do something, you say that you are
   willing to do it.

→ *collocation*
She **offered** to **help.**

∗ *noun* **offers**

1 the act of offering

→ *collocation*
I've had a **job offer.**

2 the thing or amount offered
There was an offer for their house.

→ **word family**
offering /**off**–er-ing/ *noun*
a gift
a humble offering

---

office /**off**-iss/ *noun* **offices**

1 a room or building in which business is carried on
I visited the company's head office.

2 a job, especially one in the service of the public
the office of mayor

→ *collocation*
the political party **in office**

---

official /o-**fi**-shal/

∗ *adjective*

1 having to do with an office or the duties attached to it
He has to undertake his official tasks.

2 given out or announced by those with the right to
do so
I've received official permission to visit the embassy.

∗ *noun* **officials**
a person who holds a post with certain powers or
duties

→ **word family**
officially /o-**fish**-lee/ *adverb*
formally

often /**off**-en, **off**-ten/ *adverb*
frequently
We often see them at weekends.

oil /**oil**/
* *noun* **oils**
a greasy liquid obtained from vegetable, animal, or mineral sources, and used as a food, fuel, lubricant, etc
Put more oil in the car engine.
Fry the food in sunflower oil.
* *verb* **oils, oiling, oiled**
If you oil something, you put or drop oil on it, as on the parts of a machine, to make them work smoothly.
I oiled the hinges of the gate.
➔ *word family*
oily /**oi**-lee/ *adjective*
1 covered with oil
oily hands
2 greasy
oily food

old /**oald**/ *adjective* **older, oldest**
1 not new
She wore old clothing.
2 aged
Every Thursday I read to old people.
3 belonging to the past
old customs
4 not fresh
Throw that old bread out.

on /on/

∗	*adverb*
1	being worn
➔	***collocation***
	Put your **shoes on.**
2	forward
➔	***collocation***
	They **walked on** along the path.
∗	*adjective*
	in operation
	The TV is on.
∗	*preposition*
	on top of
➔	***collocation***
	*Don't put your shoes **on the table.***

only /**oan**-lee/

∗	*adverb*
	no more than
	only two days
∗	*conjunction*
	except that
	I would love to take a holiday, only I can't afford it.
➔	***collocation***
	*She is the **only one** who can do the accounts here.*

open /o-pen/

∗	*adjective*
1	not shut, uncovered
	The gate was open.
	an open bottle
2	ready for business
	The shops are open all day Sunday.

3 not hidden
→ *collocation*
   They were very **open about** their affection for each other.
4 free from obstructions
   The road is open now.
5 public
   There is an open meeting at 6 pm.
6 sincere
   The doctor has a very open manner.
* *verb* **opens, opening, opened**
1 If you open something, you unfasten it or uncover it.
   Can you open the door?
2 to unlock
   He tried to remember the code to open the safe.
→ *phrases*
   If you are in the **open air**, you are outside.
   If you keep **open house**, you welcome all visitors.

opinion /o-**pin**-yun/ *noun* **opinions**
1 that which you think or believe about something
   Try to listen to the opinions of others.
   She has a very high opinion of herself.
2 judgment
→ *collocation*
   In the doctor's **opinion** she was too ill to work.

opportunity /op-or-**too**-ni-tee/ *noun* **opportunities**
   something that happens at the right time
→ *collocation*
   This offer is a **wonderful opportunity**.

or /**awr**/ *conjunction*

used to link alternatives
Would you like milk or orange juice?

ordeal /awr-**deel**/ *noun* **ordeals**

a difficult, painful experience
→ *collocation*
*Being taken hostage was a **terrible ordeal**.*

order /**awr**-der/

❋ *noun* **orders**
1 a methodical arrangement
→ *collocation*
Put the books **in order**.
2 a command
the officer's order
3 tidiness
There was a lack of order in the room.
4 an instruction to make or supply something
→ *collocation*
*He **placed an order** for books.*

❋ *verb* **orders, ordering, ordered**
1 If you order something, you arrange it.
Order the books alphabetically.
2 If you order someone to do something, you command it.
He ordered them to leave.
3 If you order someone or something, you give an instruction to have it made or supplied.
I ordered the paint from a company in France.

out /**out**/

❋ *adverb*
1 not inside
The children are out in the garden.

2 away

➔ *collocation*
He was told to **get out**.

＊ *preposition*
If you go out of a place or a situation, you leave it.
Get out of here!

＊ *adjective*
1 If a light is out, it is no longer shining.
2 asleep or unconscious
I went to bed and was out within minutes.

---

outside /**out**-side/

＊ *noun*
1 the outer part or parts
the outside of the building
2 the part farthest from the centre
We were standing on the outside of the group.

＊ *adjective*
1 being on the outside, external
We asked for outside help.
2 outdoor
They have an outside toilet.
3 slight
We have an outside chance of winning this game.

＊ *adverb*
on or to the outside
Let's go outside to the garden.

＊ *preposition*
on or to the exterior of, beyond
The police are outside the bank.

➔ *word family*

outsider /out-**sie**-der/ *noun*
1 a person who is not accepted as a member of a
certain group
She is still regarded as an outsider by the family.

2   someone or something that is believed to have little chance of winning
A horse regarded as an outsider won the race.

---

own /oan/
---
*   *adjective*
     belonging to yourself
     This is my own car.
*   *verb* **owns, owning, owned**
1   If you own something, you possess it.
     They own two cars.
2   to admit
     She owned that she was guilty.
→   *collocation*
     *He **owned up** to stealing the biscuits.*
→   *word family*
     owner /oa-ner/ *noun*
     someone who owns something
     ownership /oa-ner-ship/ *noun*
     the act of owning something

---

page /paidge/ *noun* **pages**
     one side of a sheet of paper in a book, etc
→   *collocation*
     ***Turn over the pages** of the magazine.*

---

pain /pain/ *noun* **pains**
1   suffering of body or mind
     the pain in his back
     the pain of her grief
→   *collocation*
     *He was **in pain** because of the injury.*

2 (**pains**) trouble, care

➔ *collocation*

*He was **at pains** to explain why he refused.*

➔ *word family*

painful /**pain**-ful/ *adjective*

used to describe something that causes pain

painless /**pain**-less/ *adjective*

used to describe something that does not cause pain

---

pair /**pair**/

∗ *noun* **pairs**

1 two things of the same kind, a set of two

She has lost a pair of gloves.

These two socks are not a pair.

2 a couple, two people, animals, etc, often one of either sex, who are thought of as being together

They have a pair of rabbits as pets.

Our neighbours are an inquisitive pair.

∗ *verb* **pairs**, **pairing**, **paired**

If you pair two things, you arrange or join them together.

➔ *collocation*

*I **paired up** all the socks.*

---

paper /**pay**-per/

∗ *noun* **papers**

1 a material made from wood pulp, rags, etc, and used for writing, printing, wrapping and many other purposes

This bin is for waste paper.

2 a newspaper

They buy a daily paper.

3   an essay

→   *collocation*
     She **wrote a paper on** *the poetry of*
     John Keats.

4   a set of examination questions on a subject or
       part of a subject
       He didn't finish the maths paper.

✳   *verb* **papers, papering, papered**
     If you paper something, you cover it with paper.
     I spent Saturday papering the walls.

part /**part**/

✳   *noun* **parts**

1   one of the pieces into which a thing can be
       divided
       I cut the cake into eight parts.

2   some but not all
       This is only a part of the toy.

3   the character played by an actor
       She always gets great parts.

✳   *verb* **parts, parting, parted**

1   If you part something, you divide it.
       I parted my hair to the left.

2   If you part from someone, you separate from
       them.
       I parted from my friends at the station.

→   *word family*
     partly /**part**-lee/ *adverb*
     in part only, not completely
     The story is only partly true.

→   *idiom*
     If you do something **part and parcel**, you do it all.

party /**par**-tee/ *noun* **parties**

1   a group of people who have the same or similar beliefs and opinions

    I am a member of a certain political party.

2   a meeting of a number of people for enjoyment

➔ *collocation*

    *We **had a** wonderful birthday **party** for my grandmother.*

    *They **threw a** great **party** for us.*

3   a person or organization taking part in something

    One of the parties involved in the crime is still missing.

---

pass /**pass**/

✱ *verb* **passes, passing, passed**

1   If you pass something, you go past it.

    You pass the church on the way to the station.

2   If you pass something to someone, you move or hand it to them.

    Could you pass the salt?

3   If time passes, it goes by.

    She got more worried as the hours passed.

4   If you pass time doing something, you spend time doing it.

    I passed time reading.

5   If one vehicle passes another on the road, it overtakes it.

6   If you pass an examination, you succeed in it.

✱ *noun* **passes**

1   success in an examination

2   a card or ticket giving entry to something

➔ *collocation*

    *He got **a pass in** maths.*

    *I have a **backstage pass** for the gig.*

past

past /past/

* *adjective*
1 gone by
   in past times
2 belonging to an earlier time
   past presidents

* *noun*
1 time gone by
   In the past he was very poor.
2 one's earlier life
   His past is unknown to his present employer.

* *preposition*
1 beyond
   The building is past the church.
2 after
   It's past three o'clock.

* *adverb*
   by
   We watched the soldiers march past.

→ *usage*
   Remember not to mix up **passed** and **past**.
   If you have **passed** something by, you are **past** that thing.

pattern /pa-tern/ *noun* **patterns**
1 a model that can be copied
   She cut the dress according to the pattern.
2 repeated examples
   There have been patterns of good behaviour.
3 a design as on cloth, a carpet, etc
   There is a lovely floral pattern on the curtains.

➔ **word family**
patterned /pa-terned/ *adjective*
covered in a pattern
We have lovely new patterned wallpaper in the hall.

pay /**pay**/

✻ *verb* **pays, paying, paid** /**paid**/

1   If you pay for goods or services, you give money
for them.
I pay the gardener for his work.

➔ *collocation*
I **paid for** my groceries.

2   If you pay for faults or crimes, you suffer for them.
Murderers must be made to pay for their crimes.

➔ **phrase**
If you **pay attention** to something, you direct your
thoughts or actions towards it.
Please pay attention!
He did not pay attention to the club's rules.

➔ *idiom*
If you **pay through the nose** for something, you
pay too much for it.
I paid through the nose for that watch and it doesn't work.

✻ *noun*
wages, salary
I get my pay on Friday.

➔ **word family**
payment /**pay**-mint/ *noun*

1   the act of paying
the payment of their debts

2   the amount paid
I received payment in full.

peace /**peess**/ noun

1   quiet, calm
    *Peace reigned in the house after the children went
    to bed.*

2   freedom from war or disorder
    The people are longing for peace.

3   the agreement to end a war
    They held peace talks.

→   **word family**
    peaceful /**peess**-ful/ *adjective*

1   quiet, calm, untroubled
    He lives in a peaceful village in the country.

2   without war
    peaceful countries

people /**pee**-pul/

*   *plural noun*

1   all those belonging to one nation or country
    the people of Brazil

2   the ordinary inhabitants of a country and not
    their rulers, etc
    The people are rebelling against their rulers.

3   persons
    There are people who care about others.

→   *usage*
    People is a plural noun. The word **peoples** is
    rarely used.
    the indigenous peoples of a country

*   *verb* **peoples, peopling, peopled**
    If a place is peopled, there are people living or
    working there.
    There are tribes who people the plains.

per /**per**/ *preposition*

1   for each
    The price is £1 per book on this stall.
2   during each
    I work 40 hours per week.
3   according to
→   *collocation*
    *I've built the shelves **as per** instructions.*

period /**pee**-ree-ud/ *noun* **periods**

1   a certain length of time
    a period of three months
2   an age in history
    the Tudor period
3   the dot or full stop marking the end of a sentence
    In American English a full stop is often called a period.
→   *usage*
    If you add 'period' after a statement, it means
    you do not want to discuss it further.
    That's the end of my argument – period!
4   in females, a time of menstruation
    I've got my period.

periodic /pee-ree-**od**-ic/ *adjective*

    happening at regular intervals
    There have been periodic breakdowns in the system.

person /**per**-sun/ *noun* **people**

    a human being, a man, woman, or child
→   *word family*
    personal /**per**-snal/ *adjective*
1   concerning a person's own private life
    These are my personal papers.

2   unkind
→   *collocation*
    *He made some **personal remarks** about her weight.*

physical /**fi**-zi-cal/ *adjective*

1   having to do with the body
    He has a physical weakness.
2   having to do with the natural world
    the physical sciences

picture /**pic**-chur/

*   *noun* **pictures**
    a painting, drawing, photograph, or other likeness, a portrait
*   *verb* **pictures, picturing, pictured**
    If you picture something, you imagine it clearly.
    Try to picture their happiness on their wedding day.

piece /**peess**/

*   *noun* **pieces**
1   a bit
    He chewed a piece of gum.
2   a distinct part
    I put the jigsaw together piece by piece.
*   *verb* **pieces, piecing, pieced**
    If you piece something together, you put it together into a whole.

place /**place**/

*   *noun* **places**
1   a particular area of space
    This park is a really nice place.
2   a village, town, etc
    My home town is a quiet place.

3   a passage in a book
➔ *collocation*
I've **lost** my **place.**

✳ *verb* **places, placing, placed**
1   If you place something somewhere, you put or set it down there.
➔ *collocation*
I **placed** my cup **on** the table top.
2   If you place someone, you recognize them.
It took me a while to place the man at the next table.

plan /plan/

✳ *noun* **plans**
1   a drawing of the outlines made by an object on the ground, a map
a plan of the building
2   a scheme of what is to happen on a future occasion
We need to make plans for the future.
✳ *verb* **plans, planning, planned**
If you plan something, you arrange beforehand what should happen.
They need to plan their future actions.
➔ *word family*
planner *noun*
someone who plans things, especially as a job

plant /plant/

✳ *noun* **plants**
1   anything growing from the earth and feeding on it through its roots
I was given lovely plants for the garden.

play

2 a factory
There is a car plant outside town.

❋ *verb* **plants, planting, planted**

1 If you plant something in the ground, you put it in there to grow.
Last year we planted potatoes.

2 If you plant something down somewhere, you set it firmly.
He planted his feet on the ground.

play /play/

❋ *verb* **plays, playing, played**

1 If you play, you amuse yourself.
The children are playing outside.

2 If you play a game or sport, you take part in it.
I like to play tennis.

3 If you play a part in a drama, you act in it.
He has been asked to play Hamlet.

4 If you play a musical instrument, you perform on it.
My sister plays the piano really well.

❋ *noun* **plays**

1 a drama
I'm going to see a play at the theatre.

2 trifling amusement or sport
The children are engaged in play.

➔ *word family*
player /**play**-er/ *noun*

1 someone who takes part in a sport or drama

2 a musical performer
The piano player entertained them for over an hour.

playful /**play**-ful/ *adjective*
fond of sport or amusement

playground /**play**-ground/ *noun*
a piece of ground set aside for children to play in

please /**pleez**/

✱ *verb* **pleases, pleasing, pleased**
1 If you please someone, you do something to make them happy or content.
He would do anything to please her.
2 If something pleases you, it seems good.
The layout of the garden pleases him enormously.
✱ *adverb*
You say please to ask if someone would be so kind as to.
Close the window, please.

plus /**plus**/

✱ *preposition*
with the addition of
brains plus beauty
✱ *adjective*
1 more than
This game is for children who are twelve plus.
2 to be added, extra
This has a plus factor.
✱ *noun*
the sign (+), used to show addition

point /**point**/

✱ *noun* **points**
1 the sharp end of anything
the point of the knife
2 a headland
I walked out to the point.

3 a dot
She added a full point to the end of the sentence.

4 the exact place or time
At what point did this happen?

5 the purpose for which something is said or written
I fail to see the point of his speech.

6 the unit of scoring in certain games
We are three points ahead.

✳ *verb* **points, pointing, pointed**

1 If you point in a direction, you show it with a finger, stick, etc.
I pointed out the house to them.

2 If you point something at something or someone, you aim it.
He pointed the gun at them.

➔ *phrases*
If you **make a point of** something, you attach special importance to it.
If you are **on the point of** doing something, you are about to do it.

➔ *word family*
pointed /**poin**-tid/ *adjective*

1 sharp
The knife has a pointed edge.

2 meant to be understood in a certain way
He made a pointed remark about her untidiness.

---

police /pu-**leess**/

✳ *plural noun*
a body of people whose job is to keep public order and see that the law is kept

→ *usage*
   Police is a plural noun.

* *verb* **polices, policing, policed**
   to make sure that law and order are kept
   They are policing the area.

policy /**pol**-i-see/ *noun* **policies**
1   the methods or plans of a government or party
    It's party policy to see this bill through.
2   a plan for a course of action
    a marketing policy
3   a written agreement with an insurance
    company
    *When they were burgled, their household insurance
    policy covered the loss of their possessions.*

political /pu-**li**-ti-cal/ *adjective*
   having to do with politics
   He has political motives for doing this.

poor /**poor**/ *adjective* **poorer, poorest**
1   having little money
    They are a very poor family.
2   unfortunate
    I feel sorry for the poor soul.
3   bad
    The weather has been particularly poor.

→ *word family*
   poorly /**poor**-lee/

* *adjective*
   an informal way of saying unwell
   I'm too poorly to go to work.

popular

* *adverb*
  badly, not well
  He performed poorly in the exam.

popular /**pop**-yu-lar/ *adjective*
1 having to do with the people
   These are the popular issues of our time.
2 well liked by most people
   She was a popular young woman.
→ *word family*
   popularity /pop-yu-**la**-ri-tee/ *noun*
   the state of being liked by most people
   popularize /**pop**-yu-la-rize/ *verb* **popularizes,
   popularizing, popularized**
   If you popularize someone or something, you
   make them or it popular.
   They are popularizing the fashion for ankle boots.

position /pu-**zi**-shun/
* *noun* **positions**
1 place
   The house was in a great position by the lake.
2 rank, grade
   He finished in second position in the race.
3 job
   He's been offered a junior position in the firm.
4 state of affairs
   Do you know about their financial position?
* *verb* **positions, positioning, positioned**
  If you position something, you place it.
  *The picture was positioned correctly on the
  wall.*

positive /**pos**-i-tiv/ *adjective*

1 sure
She was positive that she saw him.
2 certain, definite
They've had positive proof that he has left.
3 confident, optimistic
She has a very a positive manner.
4 greater than zero
Two is a positive number.
5 active, leading to practical action
some positive steps to getting fit
➜ *word family*
positively /**pos**-i-tiv-lee/ *adverb*
completely, really
This is positively the last time I'm going to do this.

possible /**paw**-si-bul/ *adjective*

1 that may be true
It is possible that she may be dead.
2 that may exist
This is possible proof.
3 that can be done
We have three possible courses of action.
➜ *word family*
possibly /**paw**-si-blee/ *adverb*
perhaps, maybe

post /**poast**/

∗ *noun* **posts**
1 a job
I'm going to seek a new post.

2   the official system by which letters, etc, are sent from one place to another
Send the parcel by first class post.

* *verb* **posts, posting, posted**
If you post a letter, you send it by post.
Have you posted the letters?

---

pound¹ /pound/ *noun* **pounds**

1   in the imperial system, a measure of weight
I've lost two pounds this week.

2   a British unit of money
a pound coin

---

pound² /pound/ *verb* **pounds, pounding, pounded**

1   If you pound something, you beat it hard.
He pounded the meat before cooking it.

2   If you pound powder or spices, you crush them.
Pound the spices into a powder.

3   If you pound the streets, you walk along them repeatedly.
He pounded the streets looking for work.

---

power /pow-er/ *noun* **powers**

1   the ability to act or do
He had lost the power of speech.

2   strength, force
He hit the rock with great power.

3   influence
She'll try to use her power on the committee.

4   control
There are too many people in his power.

5   a strong nation
the great powers of the world

6 a supply of energy, e.g. electricity
The power has gone off.
→ *word family*
powerful /**pow**-er-ful/ *adjective*
used to describe something or someone with power
powerless /**pow**-er-less/ *adjective*
used to describe something or someone without power

practical /**prac**-ti-cal/ *adjective*
1 skilful in work, able to deal with things efficiently
a practical person
2 that can be carried out, useful
Can you think of practical suggestions to help with the situation?
3 concerned with action rather than with ideas
practical help
→ *word family*
practically /**prac**-ti-ca-lee/ *adverb*
almost
practicality /prac-ti-**ca**-li-tee/ *noun*
usefulness

practice /**prac**-tiss/ *noun*
1 habit, frequent use
It was his practice to walk to work.
2 the doing of an action often to improve one's skill
piano practice
3 a doctor or lawyer's business
→ *word family*
practitioner /prac-**tish**-ner/ *noun*
someone who has a particular profession
a medical practitioner

practise

practise /**prac**-tiss/ *verb* **practise, practising, practised**

1   If you practise something, you do it frequently.
    I'm trying to practise self-control.
2   If you practise to improve your skill, you do it often.
    I'm practising the banjo.
3   If you practise a profession, you do it as your job.
    She practises medicine.

→ *usage*
    Practice is the noun and **practise** is the verb.

presence /**pre**-zinss/ *noun*

1   the state of being in the place required
    His presence was required in the business.
2   dignified or impressive appearance and bearing
    She has real presence in the room.

→ *phrase*
    If you have **presence of mind**, you have the ability to
    behave calmly in the face of difficulty or danger.

present¹ /**pre**-zent/

∗   *adjective*
1   in the place required or mentioned
    They were present at the meeting.
2   now existing or happening
    the present situation
∗   *noun*
    the time in which we live
    Think about the present and forget the past.

→ *usage*
    This sense of **present** is only used in the singular.
    You would never use **presents** when talking about
    time.

244

present²

* *noun* /**pre**-zent/ **presents**
  a gift
  I got a lot of birthday presents.

* *verb* /pre-**zent**/ **presents, presenting, presented**

1 If you present something to someone, you give or offer it.
  He presented her with flowers.

2 If you present one person to another, you introduce them.
  He presented his wife to his employer.

3 If you present a TV or radio programme you host that show.
  David is presenting a radio phone-in.

➔ *word family*
  presenter /pr-**zent**-er/ *noun*
  someone who presents something, someone who hosts a radio or TV show

---

presentable /pri-**zen**-ta-bul/ *adjective*

fit to be seen or shown
  He made himself presentable for the interview.

---

press /**press**/ *verb* **presses, pressing, pressed**

1 If you press against something, you push on or against it.
  Press the doorbell.

2 If you press something, you squeeze it.
  I was pressing grapes to make juice.

3 If you press clothes, you smooth and flatten them with an iron.
  She pressed her trousers for work.

4   If you press someone to do something, you try to persuade them to do it.
They tried to press her into joining them.

pressure /**pre**-shur/
＊   *noun* **pressures**
1   the act of pressing
➔   *collocation*
    *He **applied pressure** to the wound.*
2   forceful influence
➔   *collocation*
    *He agreed to go but only **under pressure** from his parents.*
3   stress
➔   *collocation*
    *The workers were **under pressure**.*
＊   *verb* **pressures, pressuring, pressured**
    If you pressure someone, you try to forcefully influence them into doing something.
➔   *collocation*
    *I **feel pressured** by my wife to do that course.*

pretty /**pri**-tee/
＊   *adjective* **prettier, prettiest**
    pleasing to the eye, attractive
➔   *collocation*
    *She's a **pretty girl**.*
    *She wore a **pretty dress**.*
＊   *adverb*
    quite
    The weather has been pretty good this month.

prevent /pri-**vent**/ *verb* **prevents, preventing, prevented**
    If you prevent something, you stop it from happening.

→ **collocation**
*They could not **prevent the accident**.*

→ **word family**
prevention /pri-**ven**-shun/ *noun*
the act of preventing something
Prevention is better than cure.
preventive /pri-**ven**-tiv/ *adjective*
helping to prevent something
preventive medical care

previous /**pree**-vee-us/ *adjective*
earlier, happening or existing before
his previous employer

price /**price**/ *noun* **prices**
1 the money asked or paid for something on sale
the price of a loaf of bread
2 what is required to obtain something
the price of freedom
→ **word family**
priceless /**price**-less/ *adjective*
of great value
She wore priceless jewels.

primary /**prie**-mer-ee/ *adjective*
1 first
She is in the primary stages of the disease.
2 chief
The traffic is the primary reason for his lateness.
→ **word family**
primarily /prie-**mer**-il-ee/ *adverb*
firstly, chiefly

primary school /**prie**-mer-ee skool/ *noun*
a school for young children, the first compulsory stage of education

principle /**prin**-si-pul/ *noun* **principles**

1   a general truth from which other truths follow
    I don't understand the principle of gravity.
2   a rule by which one lives
    a family with strict moral principles

private /**prie**-vit/ *adjective*

1   belonging to oneself only
    her private possessions
2   not public
    These are private houses.
3   secret
    She mistakenly read private government documents.

→   *word family*
    privatize /**prie**-vu-tize/ *verb* **privatizes, privatizing, privatized**
    If something is privatized, it is transferred from public to private ownership.
    They privatized the steel industry.
    privatization /prie-vi-tie-**zay**-shun/ *noun*
    the act of privatizing

privilege /**priv**-lidge/ *noun* **privileges**

1   a right or advantage allowed to a certain person or group only
    Members are given certain privileges.
2   advantage possessed because of social position, wealth, etc
    people of privilege

problem /**prob**-lem/ *noun* **problems**

> a question or difficulty to which the answer is hard to find
>
> *The company's problem is lack of staff.*

→ *collocation*

> *They are having big **financial problems**.*

→ *word family*

> **problematic** /prob-lem-**a**-tic/ *adjective*
> causing problems
>
> *This project has been problematic all along.*

process /**pro**-sess/ *noun* **processes**

1 the way in which a thing is done or made

> *They are using a new process to waterproof cloth.*

2 a series of actions each of which brings one nearer to the desired end

> *the production process*
> *the process of growing up*

produce

✳ *verb* /pro-**dyoos**/ **produces, producing, produced**

1 If you produce something, you bring it forward or into view.

> *He produced a handkerchief from his pocket.*

2 If something produces something else, it bears or yields it, or brings it about.

> *Trees produce rubber.*
> *The remark produced laughter.*

3 If you produce something, you make or manufacture it.

> *The factory produces furniture.*
> *The creamery produces cheese.*

product

* *noun* /**pro**-dyoos/
  things grown, crops
  fresh produce
→ *word family*
  producer /pru-**dyoo**-ser/ *noun*
1 a person or country that grows or makes certain things
2 someone who gets a play or television show ready for performance
  She works as a television producer.

product /**prod**-uct/ *noun* **products**
1 something which is made
  The factory makes wooden products.
2 result
  It's the product of much research.

production /pru-**duc**-shun/ *noun*
1 the act of making or growing
  the production of furniture
  beef production
2 the amount produced
  They have increased production.

program /**pro**-gram/
* *noun* **programs**
  a sequence of instructions put into a computer to make it perform a particular task
* *verb* **programs, programming, programmed**
  If you program a computer, you write a program for it.

programme /**pro**-gram/ *noun* **programmes**

1 a plan or scheme
   There is a programme of social reforms.
2 a list of the items in a concert, etc
   We have seen the conference programme.
3 a scheduled radio or television broadcast
→ *usage*
   The spelling **program** is always used when
   referring to computers.

progress /pru-**gress**/

* *verb* /pru-**gress**/ **progresses, progressing, progressed**
1 If you progress, you move forward.
   The line of cars progressed slowly.
2 If something progresses, it improves or
   develops.
   *The new building is progressing, although not as
   quickly as expected.*
* *noun* /**pro**-gress/
   the act of progression
   This new legislation is real progress.
→ *word family*
   progression /pru-**gre**-shun/ *noun*
1 onward movement
2 a steady and regular advance or development
   progressive /pru-**gre**-siv/ *adjective*
1 moving forward, advancing
   The progressive decline in trade was obvious.
2 believing in trying new ideas and methods
   *They teach using progressive educational
   methods.*

project

* *verb* /pro-**ject**/ **projects, projecting, projected**
1   If you project something, you throw it.
    They projected a missile into space.
2   If something projects, it sticks out.
    The sign was projecting from the wall.

* *noun* /**prodge**-ect/ **projects**
1   a plan
    a design project
    She was responsible for creation of the project.
2   a task, especially one given to a student to aid learning
    They were given a new project in class.

proper /**prop**-er/ *adjective*
1   correct, suitable, decent, polite
➔   *collocation*
    *That was a good example of **proper behaviour.***
2   thorough, complete
    That room is a proper mess.
➔   *word family*
    properly /**prop**-er-lee/ *adverb*
    correctly, suitably
    She is properly dressed for the occasion.

property /**prop**-er-tee/ *noun* **properties**
1   anything owned, that which belongs to one
    The car is his property.
2   someone's land
    They were caught trespassing on her property.
3   a quality or characteristic
    What are the properties of this chemical substance?

proportion /pru-**pore**-shun/ *noun* **proportions**

1   the size of a part when compared with the whole

➜ *collocation*

   A **large proportion** of his salary goes to pay tax.

2   the size of one object, number, etc, when compared with that of another

   The firm has a greater proportion of men to women.

3   **(proportions)** size

   They live in a house of huge proportions.

provide /pru-**vide**/ *verb* **provides, providing, provided**

1   If you provide something, you supply it.

   We are providing food for everyone.

2   If you provide for your family, you work so that they have somewhere to live, and there is money to buy food, clothes, etc.

➜ *phrase*

   If you say that someone can do something **provided that** they do another thing, you mean that they can do the first thing as long as they do the second thing as well.

public /**pu**-blic/

✳ *adjective*

1   open to all

➜ *collocation*

   *They like to sit in the **public gardens**.*

   *She takes books from the **public library**.*

2   having to do with people in general

   They have organized a public campaign.

3   well known

   She is a public figure.

purpose

✳ *noun*
the people in general
➔ *usage*
Public does not have a plural form, although it can work as both a singular and a plural noun, as in **the public has a right to know** and **the public have a right to know.**

---

purpose /**pur**-puss/ *noun* **purposes**
1   the reason for an action or a plan
➔ *collocation*
He took a journey for **business purposes**.
2   use or function
He couldn't work out the purpose of the tool.
3   determination
He is a man of purpose.
➔ *word family*
purposeful /**pur**-pus-ful/ *adjective*
1   having a clear intention in mind
She is a purposeful young woman.
2   determined
He set to work with a purposeful air.
purposely /**pur**-pus-lee/ *adverb*
intentionally, on purpose
He purposely left the gate open.

---

put /**poot**/ *verb* **puts, putting, put**
1   If you put something somewhere, you set it down or move it into a certain place.
Put the cups on the table.
I put the car in the garage.

2   If you put something to someone, you ask them.
He put a question to the speaker.

3   If you put something in words, you express it.
He put his refusal politely.

➔   *phrases*

If you **put** something **by**, you keep it for future use.

If you **put** someone **up**, you give them accommodation.

If you **put up with** something, you bear it without complaining.

---

qualify /**kwawl**-i-fie/ *verb* **qualifies, qualifying, qualified**

1   If you qualify as something, you achieve the standards required before entering a business, filling a certain position, getting a job, etc.
We were all proud when she qualified as a doctor.

2   If something qualifies someone for something, it makes them fit for it.
His low salary qualifies him for financial aid.

---

quality /**kwawl**-i-tee/ *noun* **qualities**

1   a feature of a person or thing
Critics praised the exciting quality of his writing.

➔   *collocation*

*He shows great **qualities of leadership**.*

2   the degree to which something is good or excellent, a standard of excellence
It's a low-quality paper.

---

quantity /**kwon**-ti-tee/ *noun* **quantities**

1   size, amount
the quantity of paper needed

2   a large amount
    I bought food in quantity.

race[1] /race/

*   *noun* **races**
    a contest to see who can reach a given mark in
    the shortest time
    They watched a horse race.
*   *verb* **races, racing, raced**
1   If you race, you take part in a race.
2   If you race, you run or move very quickly
    She raced to catch the bus.

race[2] /race/ *noun* **races**

1   any of the main groups into which human
    beings can be divided according to their physical
    characteristics
2   the fact of belonging to one of these groups
    They were wrong to discriminate on the grounds of
    race.
3   a group of people who share the same culture,
    language, etc
    the German race
4   ancestors, family

radio /**ray**-dee-o/ *noun* **radios**

1   the sending or receiving of sounds through the
    air by electric waves
2   an apparatus for receiving sound broadcast
    through the air by electric waves
3   the radio broadcasting industry
    a career in radio

rate /rate/

* *noun* **rates**

1 the amount of one thing measured by its relation to another

The death rate is the number of people who die yearly to every thousand of the population.

2 speed

My heart rate has increased dramatically.

3 price

→ *collocation*

*They were charged at an unfair **daily rate**.*

* *verb* **rates, rating, rated**

1 If you rate something or someone, you assess its or their quality or worth.

I rate it as the worst café in town.

2 If you rate someone or something, you think they are of a great standard.

We really rate him as a plumber.

I don't rate that café at all, its coffee is very poor.

rather /ra-ther/ *adverb*

1 preferably, more willingly

She would rather die than leave.

2 fairly, quite

She is rather talented.

3 more exactly, more truly

She is thoughtless rather than cruel.

reach /reech/

verb **reaches, reaching, reached**

1 If you reach something out, you stretch out.

He reached out a hand.

2   If you reach out for something, you stretch out a hand or arm for some purpose.
She reached for a book.

3   If you reach somewhere, you arrive there.
He reached the summit of the mountain.

→   *collocation*
*He finally **reached a decision.***

*   *noun* **reaches**

1   the distance you can extend the hand from the body.
The telephone was within reach.

2   a distance that can be easily travelled
The airport is within easy reach.

---

read /reed/ *verb* **reads, reading, read** /red/

1   If you read something written, you look at it and understand what it means.
Try and read the instructions.

→   *collocation*
***Read out** the message in the letter.*

2   When a computer reads data, it extracts it from a storage system.

→   *word family*
readable /**ree**-da-bul/ *adjective*
easy to read, interesting

---

ready /**re**-dee/ *adjective*

prepared and fit for use
I'm so glad that dinner is ready.

→   *word family*
readiness /**ree**-dee-ness/ *noun*
the state of being ready

real /**reel**/ *adjective*

1   actually existing

➔ *collocation*

    *It happens in **real life**.*

2   true, genuine, not false or fake

    It looks like real gold.

really /**ree**-lee/ *adverb*

1   actually, in fact

➔ *collocation*

    *This describes things **as they really are**.*

2   very

    They had a really pleasant day.

reason /**ree**-zun/

✳ *noun* **reasons**

1   cause for acting or believing

    He wondered about the reason for her sadness.

2   the power to think things out

    He has lost his reason.

3   good sense

➔ *collocation*

    *He wouldn't **listen to reason**.*

✳ *verb* **reasons, reasoning, reasoned**

1   If you reason, you think something out step by step.

    We reasoned that they would attack at dawn.

2   If you reason with someone, you try to convince them by arguing.

    Can you reason them into being less hasty?

➔ *word family*

    reasonable /**reez**-na-bul/ *adjective*

1   sensible

    It was a reasonable suggestion.

2 willing to listen to another's arguments
He's a reasonable person.

3 not excessive
It seems like a reasonable price.

---

receive /ri-**seev**/ *verb* **receives, receiving, received**

1 If you receive something, you come into possession of it.

→ *collocation*
I **received a letter** on Thursday.
He's just **received** good **news**.

2 If you receive people, you welcome them.

→ *collocation*
We're ready to **receive guests.**

---

recent /**ree**-sint/ *adjective*

not long past

→ *collocation*
We've been trying to keep up with **recent events.**
The **recent developments** have been shocking.

→ *word family*
recently /**ree**-sint-lee/ *adverb*
done in recent times
The house was built recently.

---

record

✱ *verb* /ri-**cawrd**/ **records, recording, recorded**

1 If you record something in writing, you write it down.
They recorded the score in a notebook.

2 If you record sounds or images, you preserve them by mechanical means, on a CD, tape, etc.
Did you record your sister singing in the concert?
I recorded the TV show.

* *noun* /**reh**-curd/ **records**

1 a recorded account

➜ *collocation*
   Is this **on the record?**

2 a book containing written records, a register
   These details are found in the parish records.

3 the best performance yet known in any type of contest

➜ *collocation*
   He's **beaten** all **the records.**

4 what is known about a person's past
   She has a good work record.

5 a history of being arrested and charged by the police
   His record was well known to the police.

---

red /**red**/

* *adjective*

1 of a colour like blood
   She wears a red coat.
   His hands are red with cold.

2 of a colour that varies between a golden brown and a reddish brown
   She has beautiful red hair.

* *noun*
   the colour red

➜ *idiom*
   If you **see red**, you become suddenly very angry.

---

reduce /ri-**dyooss**/ *verb* **reduces, reducing, reduced**

1 If you reduce something, you make it less, smaller, or less heavy.

→ **collocation**
The shop has been **reducing prices.**
The lorry must **reduce its load.**

2   If you are reduced to a certain state, you are
    brought or forced to do something less pleasant,
    worthy, etc, than usual.
    He has been reduced to begging on the streets.

→ **word family**
reduction /ri-**duc**-shun/ *noun*
something that has been reduced, or the amount
by which something has been reduced

---

region /**ree**-jun/ *noun* **regions**

1   a part of a country, often a large area of land
    the coastal region
2   neighbourhood, area
    He has a pain in the region of his kidney.
    Unemployment is now in the region of two million.

→ **word family**
regional /**reej**-nal/ *adjective*
connected with or related to a region or regions

---

regular /**re**-gyu-lar/

∗   *adjective*
1   normal, usual
    This is his regular route to work.
2   done always in the same way or at the same time
    He doesn't like to disrupt his regular habits.
3   occurring, acting, etc, with equal amounts of
    space, time, etc, between

→ **collocation**
*He checked for a **regular pulse.***

*Guards were placed at **regular intervals.***

4 the same on both or all sides
The girl had regular features.

5 ordinary, normal
He's just a regular guy.

✳ *noun* **regulars**
a habitual customer
one of the local pub's regulars

➔ **word family**
regularity /re-gyu-**la**-ri-tee/ *noun*
the state of being regular
regularly /**re**-gyu-lar-lee/ *adverb*
often

---

relevant /**re**-li-vant/ *adjective*

having to do with the matter under consideration
We need to discuss matters relevant to the situation.

➔ **word family**
relevance /**re**-li-vanse/ *noun*
the state of being relevant

---

remain /ri-**main**/

✳ *verb* **remains, remaining, remained**

1 If you remain in one place, you stay there.

➔ *collocation*
*She asked to **remain in** the house.*

2 If you have something remaining, you have it left over.
A little money remained after the bills were paid.

3 If something remains in a state, it continues to be that way.
They remained friends despite their argument.

✳ *plural noun* **remains** /ri-mainz/
1 that which is left
   the remains of the meal
2 a dead body
   They buried his remains this afternoon.
➔ **word family**
   remainder /ri-**main**-der/ *noun*
   that which is left over or behind
   the remainder of the evening

remember /ri-**mem**-ber/ *verb* **remembers, remembering, remembered**

1 If you remember something, you keep it in mind.
   She remembered her youth with pleasure.
2 If you try to remember something, you recall it to your mind.
   I tried to remember his name.
3 If you ask to be remembered to someone, you give greetings to them through another person.
➔ *collocation*
   Remember me to your father.

report /ri-**poart**/

✳ *verb* **reports, reporting, reported**
1 If you report something as news or information, you tell it.
   The paper reported a new medical development.
2 If you report an account of something, you write it, especially for a newspaper or website.
➔ *collocation*
   Many newspapers **have reported** *this story.*
3 If you report someone for something, you make a

complaint about them for having done wrong.
She reported the boys who were fighting in the playground.

* *noun* **reports**
1 a spoken or written account of work performed by a committee, a student, etc
2 an account of something that has been said or done, especially when written for a newspaper or website
3 a rumour
There were reports that he had married.

→ *word family*
reporter /ri-**poar**-ter/ *noun*
a person who reports for a newspaper or television or radio broadcast

---

require /ri-**kwire**/ *verb* **requires, requiring, required**
1 If you require something, you need it.
→ *collocation*
*We have **all we require** to make the meal.*
2 If you are required to do something, you must do it by demand or order.
The children are required to attend school.
→ *word family*
requirement /ri-**kwire**-ment/ *noun*
1 a need, something needed
The shop is able to supply all our requirements.
2 a necessary condition
the minimum requirement for entry to university

---

research /ree-**search**/ *noun*
careful study to discover new facts

respect

→ **collocation**
*Her son has been engaged in **medical research** for many years.*

→ **usage**
There is no plural form of **research**.

---

respect /ri-**spect**/
---
* *verb* **respects, respecting, respected**
1 If you respect someone, you think highly of them.
→ **collocation**
*The critics **respect** him **as** a writer.*
2 If you respect something, you pay attention to it, and act according to it.
You must respect their wishes.
* *noun*
honour
Please treat older people with respect.
→ **word family**
respects /ri-**spects**/ *plural noun*
good wishes
He sent his respects to the old man.

---

responsible /ri-**spon**-si-bul/ *adjective*
---
1 able to be trusted
They are responsible members of staff.
2 having to say or explain what you have done
He is responsible for his actions.
3 being the cause of something
Who is responsible for this mess?
→ **word family**
responsibility /ri-spon-si-**bi**-li-tee/ *noun*
something that you must be in charge of or look after
Walking the dog is your responsibility.

responsibly /ri-**spon**-sib-lee/ *adverb*
in a trustworthy way

rest¹ /rest/

✳ *noun* **rests**
1 a pause in work
I would like a rest from digging.
2 inactivity
He has had quite a rest.
3 sleep
a good night's rest
4 a support or prop
He was tired and used the wall as a rest.

✳ *verb* **rests, resting, rested**
1 If you rest from action or work, you stop for a time.
Let me rest for a few minutes.
2 If you rest, you are still or quiet.
The young children are resting.
3 If you rest on something, you are supported by it.
➔ *collocation*
*His feet are **resting on** the table.*

rest² /rest/ *noun*

(usually **the rest**) that which is left, the remainder
Would you like the rest of this cake?

result /ri-**zult**/

✳ *noun* **results**
1 that which happens as the effect of something
else, the outcome
➔ *collocations*
*Have you heard **the results of** the election?*
*He broke his leg **as a result** of the accident.*

2 the final score in a sports contest.

* *verb* **results, resulting, resulted**

1 If something results from something else, it follows as the effect of that thing.

➜ *collocation*

His blindness **results from** the accident.

2 If something results in something else, it ends in it.

➜ *collocation*

The research **resulted in** a new drug on the market.

return /ri-**turn**/

* *verb* **returns, returning, returned**

1 If you return somewhere, you come or go back.

➜ *collocation*

They **returned to** the house.

2 If you return something, you give or send it back.

He returned his present unopened.

* *noun* **returns**

1 a coming or going back

➜ *collocation*

It was after their **return from** holiday.

2 what is given or sent back

➜ *collocation*

They asked for the **return of** the library books.

3 profit

It was a good return from their investment.

4 a written statement of certain facts, expenses, figures, etc

They filled in their annual tax return.

review /ri-**vyoo**/

* *verb* **reviews, reviewing, reviewed**

1 If you review something, you look over it

again or consider it with a view to changing it.

He thought about reviewing the situation.

2 If you review books, plays, films, etc, you write your opinion of them.

* noun **reviews**

1 a looking back on the past
a review of the year's news

2 reconsideration or revision
a review of company policy

3 an article in a newspaper, magazine, etc, giving an opinion on a book, play, etc
a review of the latest movie

---

rich /rich/ *adjective* **richer, richest**

1 having much money, wealthy
He's a very rich man.

2 fertile
This land has rich soil.

3 plentiful
This is a rich source of gold.

4 containing much fat or sugar
This sauce is too rich for me.

5 deep, strong
a rich singing voice
rich colours

➔ *word family*

richness /rich-ness/ *noun*
the state of being rich

riches /ri-chiz/ *plural noun*
wealth

richly /rich-lee/ *adverb*

1 in a rich manner
She was richly dressed.

2 with riches
The children were richly rewarded.

right /rite/

✳ *adjective*
1 correct
They won't tell us the right answer.
2 true
Is it right to say he left early?
3 just, morally correct
It is not right to let him go unpunished.
4 straight
Go right ahead.
5 on the side of the right hand
Stand at her right side.
6 in good condition
Call a plumber to put the washing machine right.
7 suitable, appropriate
the right person for the job

✳ *verb* **rights, righting, righted**
If you right something, you put it back in position.
I righted the vase on the mantelpiece.

✳ *noun* **rights**
1 that which is correct, good, or true
They are in the right.
2 something to which you have a just claim
Freedom of speech is a right.
3 When you look at the word *it*, the letter *t* is on the right the side, opposite to the left.
He was standing on her right.

* *adverb*

1 straight
   Go right home.

2 exactly, correctly
   I did everything right.

3 to the right-hand side
   Move right, please.

rise /**rize**/ *verb* **rises, rising, rose**, **risen** /**ri**-zin/

1 If you rise, you get up from bed.
   I always rise early.

2 If you rise from something, you stand up.
   She rose from the chair to go.

3 If something rises, it goes upwards.
   Smoke was rising from the chimney.

4 If a price rises, it increases.
   Fuel costs are rising.

➔ *phrases*
   If something **gives rise to** something, it causes or brings it about.
   If you **rise to the occasion**, you do all that is necessary at a difficult time.
   If you **take a rise out of** someone, you play a joke or trick on them.

➔ *word family*
   rising /**rie**-zing/ *noun*
   the act of rising

risk /**risk**/

* *noun* **risks**

1 danger

2 possible harm or loss

* *verb* **risks, risking, risked**

1   If you risk something or someone, you put it or them in danger.
→   **collocations**
    *He is **risking his health**.*
    *She **risked her life** to save the puppy.*
2   If you risk something, you take the chance of something bad or unpleasant happening.
→   **collocations**
    *He **risked defeat**.*
    *He **risks losing** his business.*
→   **word family**
    risky /**ri**-skee/ *adjective*
    dangerous
    a risky journey

river /**ri**-ver/ *noun* **rivers**
    a large running stream of water

road /**road**/ *noun* **roads**
1   a prepared public way for travelling on
    The road was icy.
2   a street
    He lives in the next road.
3   a way
    the road to success

role /**role**/ *noun* **roles**
1   the part played by an actor
    He played the role of Hamlet.
2   actions or duties
    What is his role in the company?

room /room/ *noun* **rooms**

1   a walled space within a house or other building
    There are three rooms upstairs.
2   space
    There's room for three in the back of the car.
3   space for free movement
    There's no room to dance.
4   scope
    There's room for improvement.

→ **word family**
    roomy /roo-mee/ *adjective*
    having plenty of space
    a roomy car

round /round/ *adjective*

*   *adjective* **rounder, roundest**
    like a ball or circle in shape
*   *noun* **rounds**
1   a round object
    Cut a round from that pastry.
2   a duty visit to all the places under your care
    The doctor was doing his rounds.
3   a spell or outburst
    There was a round of applause.
*   *adverb*
1   in the opposite direction
→ *collocation*
    *He **turned round**.*
2   in a circle
    The field is fenced all round.
3   from one person to another
→ *collocation*
    *They **passed** the wine **round**.*

4 from place to place
I drive round all night.

✳ *preposition*

1 on every side of
The members sit round the table.

2 with a circular movement about
They plan to sail round the world.

✳ *verb* **rounds, rounding, rounded**

1 If you round something, you give a round shape to it.
He rounded the corners with sandpaper.

2 If you round something, you go around it.
The ships rounded the headland.

---

run /**run**/

✳ *verb* **runs, running, ran, run**

1 If you run, you move quickly on foot.
He ran to catch the bus.

2 If something runs, it moves from one place to another.
This train runs from Paris to Venice.

3 If something runs through or from something, it flows through or from it.
Blood was running from the wound.

4 If you run something, you organize or manage it.
She runs the local branch of the company.

5 If something runs for a certain amount of time, it lasts or continues for that time.
The play is running for a year.

✳ *noun* **runs**

1 act of running
I'll go for a run in the morning.

2 the length of time for which something runs

→ *collocation*
*The play has **a run of** six months.*

3 a widespread demand for

→ *collocation*
*There has been a **run on** umbrellas.*

4 an enclosed place for animals or fowls
The chickens are in their run.

→ *phrases*
If you **run someone down**, you say bad things about them.

If you **run someone over**, you knock them over in a vehicle.

If something is **run down**, it is worn out or in need of repair.

safe /safe/

✳ *adjective* **safer, safest**

1 out of harm or danger
The children are safe in bed.

2 not likely to cause harm, danger, or risk
This is safe to eat.

✳ *noun* **safes**
a strong box or room for valuables

→ *word family*
safely *adverb*
If you do something safely, you do it so it does not cause harm.

sale /sale/ *noun* **sales**

1 the act of selling

2 the exchange of anything for money

3 a selling of goods more cheaply than usual
I was hoping to buy something in the January sales.

same /same/

* *adjective*

in no way different

➔ *collocations*

*I'd always thought that they were **the same person**.*
*I keep making the **same mistake**.*

* *noun*

the same person or thing

I'll have the same.

* *adverb*

in a like manner

➔ *word family*

sameness /**same**-ness/ *noun*

lack of change or variety

She hated the sameness of the canteen food.

say /say/

* *verb* **says, saying, said** /sed/

1 to utter in words, to speak

He said that the boat would be late and it was.

2 to state

Can you say what you mean?

➔ *usage*

You say something to someone, or tell
someone something, but you do not say
someone something.

* *noun*

the right to give an opinion

You can have your say in a minute.

➔ *word family*

saying /**say**-ing/ *noun*

a proverb, something commonly said

scale /scale/

* *noun* **scales**

1 a series of successive musical notes between one note and its octave
practise your scales

2 the size of a map compared with the amount of area it represents
a scale of ten miles to the inch

3 a measure
the scale on a thermometer

4 a system of units for measuring
the decimal scale

5 a system of grading
the social scale

6 size, extent
They like to entertain on a large scale.

* *verb* **scales, scaling, scaled**
If you scale a building or wall, you climb it.

scene /seen/ *noun* **scenes**

1 the place where something happens
the scene of the crime

2 what a person can see from a certain viewpoint
What a beautiful scene from our window.

3 a distinct part of a play
Let's rehearse the third scene of Act 2.

4 a quarrel or open show of strong feeling in a public place
Please don't make a scene.

➔ *phrase*
If something is done **behind the scenes**, it is done in private.

➔ *word family*
scenery /**seen**-ree/ *noun*

1 the painted backgrounds set up during a play to represent the places of the action
2 the general appearance of a countryside
This is an area of beautiful scenery.
scenic /**see**-nic/ *adjective*
1 having to do with scenery
2 beautiful to look at

scheme /skeem/

✻ *noun* **schemes**
1 a plan of what is to be done
We have a good scheme at work.
2 a plot
There was a scheme to kill the president.
✻ *verb* **schemes, scheming, schemed**
If you scheme something, you plan or plot it.
➔ *word family*
schemer /**skee**-mer/ *noun*
someone who schemes
scheming /**skee**-ming/ *adjective*
given to planning schemes

school /skool/

✻ *noun* **schools**
1 a place where instruction is given, where people learn
2 a group of writers, thinkers, painters, etc, having the same or similar methods, principles, aims, etc
✻ *verb* **schools, schooling, schooled**
If you school someone in something, you train

them to have a certain skill or knowledge.
She was well schooled in European politics.

→ **word family**
schooling /**skoo**-ling/ *noun*
training or education

science /**sie**-ense/ *noun* sciences

1 all that is known about a subject, arranged in a systematic manner
   the science of geography
2 the study of the laws and principles of nature
   I am interested in biology, physics, and other branches of science.

sea /**see**/ *noun* seas

1 (no plural) the salt water that covers much of the Earth's surface
2 a large area of salt water
   the North Sea
3 a large amount or extent of anything
   There is a sea of papers on her desk.

→ **phrase**
If you say that you are **at sea,** you are on the sea.

→ **idiom**
If you say that you are **all at sea about** something, you are confused about it.

search /serch/

✳ *verb* **searches, searching, searched**
If you search for someone or something, you try to find them or it.

* *noun* **searches**

the act of looking for something

→ *word family*

searcher /**ser**-cher/ *noun*

someone who searches for something

search engine /**serch en**-jin/ *noun*

computer software designed to locate items on a given topic on the internet

searching /**ser**-ching/ *adjective*

thorough, testing thoroughly

a searching interview

---

season¹ /**see**-zun/ *noun* **seasons**

1 one of the four divisions of the year: winter, spring, summer, and autumn

2 a time of the year noted for a particular activity

The football season starts soon.

→ *word family*

seasonable /**seez**-na-bul/ *adjective*

1 happening at the right time

seasonable advice

2 suitable to the season of the year

seasonable weather

seasonal /**seez**-nal/ *adjective*

having to do with one or all of the seasons

seasonal variations in the weather

---

season² /**see**-zun/ *verb* **seasons, seasoning, seasoned**

If you season food, you add something to it to give it a good taste.

→ *word family*

seasoning /**seez**-ning/ *noun*

anything added to food to improve its taste

second¹ /**se**-cund/

* *adjective*

coming immediately after first

I was second in the race.

* *noun* **seconds**

1 (no plural) a person who comes after the first person

2 (**seconds**) goods that are sold more cheaply because of some flaw

* *verb* **seconds, seconding, seconded**

If you second someone, you support them.

I seconded her as treasurer.

second² /**se**-cund/ *noun* **seconds**

1 one sixtieth of a minute

I'll be there in a few seconds.

2 a very small amount of time

Just a second!

second³ /si-**cond**/ *verb* **seconds, seconding, seconded**

If someone is seconded, they are transferred temporarily from normal duties to other duties.

He has been seconded to the advertising department for a month.

➔ *word family*

secondary /**se**-cun-de-ree/ *adjective*

of less importance

These are secondary considerations.

section /**sec**-shun/ *noun* **sections**

1 a distinct part of something

the finance section of the company

2 a part that has been cut off
Would you like a section of this apple?

sector /**sec**-tor/ *noun* **sectors**

1 one of the parts into which an area is divided
They live in the Italian sector of the city.

2 part of a field of activity
He works in the banking sector.

3 a section of a circle
A sector of a circle looks like a pizza slice.

see /see/ *verb* **sees, seeing, saw /saw/, seen**

1 If you see something, you look at it with your eyes.
I saw the lake from the top of the hill.

2 If you see something, you notice it.
I didn't see the police car.

3 If you ask whether someone sees something, you are asking if they understand it.
Do you see what I mean?

4 If you go to see someone, you visit them.
I went to see my aunt yesterday.

➔ *phrases*

If you **see about** something, you attend to it.

If you **see something off**, you get rid of it.

If you **see something through**, you keep on with it until it is complete.

em /seem/ *verb* **seems, seeming, seemed**

If you seem to be something, you appear to be).

seems to be happy about the situation.

→ *word family*
seeming /**see**-ming/ *adjective*
having the appearance of, apparent
His seeming honesty misled her.

---

sell /**sell**/ *verb* **sells, selling, sold** /**soald**/

If you sell something, you give it in exchange for money.

→ *word family*
seller /**se**-ler/ *noun*
a person who sells

---

send /**send**/ *verb* **sends, sending**, **sent** /**sent**/

If you send something, you arrange for it to be taken from one place to another.
I am sending you a package today.

→ *word family*
sender /**sen**-der/ *noun*
someone who sends something

---

senior /**seen**-yur/

* *adjective*
1 older
2 higher in rank or importance
a senior partner in the firm
* *noun* **seniors**
1 a person who is older
She is her brother's senior.
2 a person having longer service or higher rank
Her seniors in the firm are having a meeting.

→ *word family*
seniority /seen-**yawr**-i-tee/ *noun*
the state of being senior

sense /senss/

* *noun* **senses**

1 any one of the five faculties – sight, hearing, taste, smell, and touch – by which people and animals gain knowledge of things outside themselves

2 wisdom in everyday things
   At least have the sense to keep warm.

3 understanding
   He has no sense of direction.

4 meaning
   The word has several senses.

* *verb* **senses, sensing, sensed**
If you sense something, you feel it or you are aware of it.
He sensed her presence in the room
She sensed danger and ran away.

separate

* *verb* /**sep**-a-rate/ **separates, separating, separated**

1 If you separate two things, you pull them apart.
   I separated the two pieces of paper.

2 If you separate from your friends, you go away from them.
   We separated at the train station.

3 If people in a relationship separate, they stop living together and end the relationship.
   Her parents have separated.

* *adjective* /**sep**-rut/
unconnected, distinct, apart

→ *word family*
separable /se-pra-bul/ *adjective*
used to describe things that can be separated

separation /se-pe-**ray**-shun/ *noun*
1 act of separating
2 an agreement by a married couple to end their marriage and live apart from each other

series /**see**-reez/ *noun* **series**
a number of things arranged in a definite order

serious /**see**-ree-us/ *adjective*
1 thoughtful
Her father was in a serious mood.
2 important
There are more serious issues.
3 likely to cause danger
It was a serious wound.

service /**ser**-viss/ *noun* **services**
1 the work of a servant or employee
She has five years' service with the company.
2 use, help
These people can be of service to us.
3 a religious ceremony
4 in tennis, the hit intended to put the ball into play

set /set/
* *verb* **sets, setting, set**
1 If you set something somewhere, you put it there.
Did you set your glasses on the table?
2 If you set something in place, you fix it in position.
The doctor set the broken bone.
3 If the sun sets, it sinks below the horizon.

* *noun* **sets**

1 a number of things of the same kind
a chess set

2 a group of people with similar interests
the rugby set

3 a group of games in a tennis match
She was beaten by two sets to one.

* *adjective*
fixed, regular
a set routine

phrase
If you **set off** or **set out**, you begin a journey.

---

several /**sev**-ral/ *adjective*

more than two, but not very many
He gave several reasons for turning down the job.

---

sex /**seks**/

* *noun*

1 the state of being male or female
the battle of the sexes

2 the qualities by which an animal or plant is seen
to be male or female
We found out the sex of the rabbit.

3 sexual intercourse

→ **collocation**
*to **have sex***

→ **usage**
Sex, sense **3**, is used in the singular; not **sexes**.

* *verb* **sexes, sexing, sexed**
If you sex an animal you examine it to find out
whether it is male or female.
The vet sexed the rabbits. They were all female.

shall /**shall**/ *verb*

If you say that you shall do something, you mean that you intend to do it.

I shall pay the lawyer.

shape /**shape**/

✷ *noun* **shapes**

the form or outline of anything

clouds of different shapes

✷ *verb* **shapes, shaping, shaped**

If you shape something, you form it.

I shaped the sand into a castle.

This early decision shaped his career.

➔ *phrase*

If you are **in good shape**, you are in good physical condition.

➔ *word family*

shapeless /**shape**-less/ *adjective*

ugly or irregular in shape

She was wearing a shapeless brown dress.

shapely /**shape**-lee/ *adjective*

attractive in shape

shapely legs

share /**share**/

✷ *noun* **shares**

1   part of a thing belonging to a particular person

our share of the bill

2   one of the equal parts of the money of a company or business, lent by people who may then receive a part of the profits

3   the cutting part of a plough

✳ *verb* **shares, sharing, shared**
If you share something, you divide it up so that a number of people get a part of it.

she /**shee**/ *pronoun*

the woman, girl, or female animal referred to earlier
Mary loves dogs, so she's buying a puppy.

➔ *word family*
her *pronoun*
referring to a female person or animal
Mary loves her dog.
herself *pronoun*
reflexive form of **she**
Mary bought the dog for herself.
hers *determiner*
associated with **her**
That dog is hers.

shop /**shop**/

✳ *noun* **shops**
1 a place where goods are sold
➔ *collocations*
*She works at a **flower shop**.*
*I went to the **corner shop**.*
2 a place where work is done with tools or machines
The car is in the shop.
✳ *verb* **shops, shopping, shopped**
If you shop, you visit shops to buy things.
➔ *collocation*
*I went **shopping for** groceries.*

→ *phrase*
If you **talk shop**, you talk about work.

---

short /shawrt/ *adjective* **shorter, shortest**

1   not long or tall
She is quite short in height.
→ *collocation*
*It's only a **short distance**.*
2   not enough
short measures
3   without enough of
→ *collocation*
*I'm **short of** money just now.*
4   not lasting long
It was a short holiday.
5   quick and almost impolite
She was very short on the phone.
→ *word family*
shorts *plural noun*
trousers reaching not lower than the knees
shortly /shawrt-lee/ *adverb*
briefly, soon
shortage /shawr-tidge/ *noun*
a lack of, not enough of
→ *collocation*
*There is a **staff shortage**.*
→ *phrase*
If you say something **in short**, you say it in a few words.

---

should /shood/ *verb*

used to express duty, what a person is supposed to do
He should be at work today but he has stayed at home.

show /shoa/

* *verb* **shows, showing, showed**

1   If you show something, you let it be seen, or display it.
She showed them the new car.

2   If you show someone the way, you point it out.
Can you please show them the way to the exit?

3   If something shows, it is in sight.
There was a light showing under the door.

* *noun* **shows**

1   a display

2   a performance or entertainment
Get tickets for the show.

3   a gathering at which flowers, animals, etc, are displayed to the public
I'm going to the agricultural show at the weekend.

sign /sine/

* *noun* **signs**

1   a mark, movement, gesture, etc, representing an accepted meaning
She gave a sign that she agrees.

2   a notice to give directions or advertise

➔   *collocation*
*There are several broken **shop signs** in the street.*

* *verb* **signs, signing, signed**

1   If you sign something, you write your name on it.

➔   *collocation*
*I asked him to **sign the agreement**.*

2   to convey meaning by a movement of the head, hands, etc
He signed to his deaf daughter using his hands.

significant /sig-**ni**-fi-cant/ *adjective*

full of meaning, important

➜ *collocations*

*There has been **no significant change** in the patient's condition.*

*These are **significant events**.*

similar /**si**-mi-lar/ *adjective*

like, resembling

They have similar attitudes.

➜ *word family*

similarity /si-mi-**la**-ri-tee/ *noun*

likeness, resemblance

There was some similarity in their attitude.

simple /**sim**-pul/ *adjective* **simpler, simplest**

1 unmixed, without anything added, pure

It is the simple truth.

2 not complicated

➜ *collocation*

*There must be a **simple explanation**.*

3 plain

She was wearing a simple dress.

4 trusting, innocent, and inexperienced

We are simple country boys.

since /**sinse**/

* *preposition*

from a certain time till now

He's been really unhappy since leaving school.

* *conjunction*

1 from the time that

It's some time since we saw you.

2 because
Since we are friends, I'll tell you my secret.

single /**sing**-gul/

* *adjective*
1 one only, alone
a single sheet of paper
2 unmarried or not in a relationship
I have several single friends.

* *verb* **singles, singling, singled**
If you single someone out, you pick them for special attention, etc.
She was singled out from all the other candidates.

→ *word family*
single-handed /sing-gul-**han**-did/ *adjective*
without help, done or working alone
single-minded /sing-gul-**mine**-did/ *adjective*
concentrating on one main purpose

sit /**sit**/ *verb* **sits, sitting, sat**

1 If you sit, you take a rest on a seat.
I sat down on the sofa.
2 If you sit something on something else, you rest it upon it.
I sat my suitcase on the bed.

→ *phrase*
If you **sit up**, you sit with your back straight up.

site /**site**/ *noun* **sites**

the ground on which a building or a number of buildings stands or is to stand
They have chosen a site for the new school.

situation /si-chu-**way**-shun/ *noun* **situations**

1   a place or position
The house is in a lovely situation.

2   a job
I'm seeking a new situation.

3   circumstances
I don't know about their financial situation.

---

size /size/

＊   *noun* **sizes**
bigness, bulk, the physical proportions of something

＊   *verb* **sizes, sizing, sized**

1   If you size various things, you arrange them in order according to size.
She was sizing the eggs to sell them.

2   If you size something, you make it fit.
You'll need to size the sofa cover to fit properly.

＊   *phrase*
If you **size something up**, you form an opinion about it.

---

skin /skin/

＊   *noun* **skins**

1   the natural outer covering of animals

2   a thin layer or covering
A skin formed on top of the rice pudding.

＊   *verb* **skins, skinning, skinned**
If you skin something, you remove its skin.

➔   *word family*
skinny /**skin**-ee/ *adjective*
very thin

sleep /sleep/

* *verb* **sleeps, sleeping, slept**
  If you sleep, you rest your body, with the eyes shut, unaware of your surroundings.
* *noun* **sleeps**
  a complete rest for the body, as at night
  We had a good sleep last night.

→ **word family**
  sleepily /**slee**-pi-lee/ *adverb*
  in a drowsy, sleepy manner
  sleeper /**slee**-per/ *noun*
1 a person or animal who is asleep
2 a long rectangular block that supports railway lines
3 a coach on a train with bunks for sleeping passengers
  sleeping bag /**slee**-ping bag/ *noun*
  a large, warmly lined, zipped bag in which a person can sleep, especially outdoors
  sleeping pill /**slee**-ping pill/ *noun*
  a drug that makes a person sleepy and drowsy, so as to help him or her to sleep
  sleepless /**sleep**-less/ *adjective*
1 unable to sleep
  I lay sleepless all night.
2 without sleep
  a sleepless night
  sleepwalker /**sleep**-waw-ker/ *noun*
  a person who walks about in his or her sleep
  sleepy /**slee**-pee/ *adjective*
  wanting to sleep, drowsy
  The sleepy little girl was ready for bed.

small /smawl/

---

* *adjective* **smaller, smallest**

1 little
The children are so small.

2 young
There's free admission for small children.

3 not much
There's small reason to rejoice.

* *noun*
the lower part of the back

smile /smile/

---

* *verb* **smiles, smiling, smiled**
If you smile, you show joy, amusement, etc, by an upward movement of the lips.

➔ *collocation*
She **smiled at** me.

* *noun* **smiles**
a look of pleasure or amusement

so /so/

---

* *adverb*

1 in this or that manner
I like my coffee strong – could you please make it so?

2 to that extent
It was so wet that we stayed in.

3 thus
She was tired so left the party.

4 very
I'm so happy.

* *conjunction*
in order that
Be quiet so I can think.

social /**so**-shal/ adjective
1 having to do with society
   There are many social problems.
2 living in an organized group
   We are very social creatures.
➔ *word family*
   sociable /**so**-sha-bl/ adjective
   friendly, good with people

society /su-**sie**-u-tee/ noun **societies**
1 a group of people living together in a single organized community
2 a group of people who meet regularly for a special purpose, mixing with other people
   a debating society
3 the wealthy or high-ranking members of a community

software /**soft**-ware/ noun
   the programs used in computers
➔ *usage*
   Software is used with both as singular and plural verbs but you would never say **softwares**.

solution /su-**loo**-shun/ noun **solutions**
1 a liquid containing another substance dissolved in it
   a salty solution
2 the answer to or explanation of a problem, etc
   the solution to a crossword puzzle

son /**sun**/ noun **sons**
   a male child
   I have three sons and a daughter.

soon /**soon**/ *adverb*

1   in a short time
They'll be here soon.

2   early
It's too soon to know.

3   willingly
I would just as soon go.

sorry /**sor**-ee/ *adjective*

1   feeling pity or regret, sad because of wrongdoing
He's sorry for what he has done.

2   wretched
You are a sorry sight in your muddy clothes.

sort /**sawrt**/

∗   *noun* **sorts**
a kind, class, or set
a new sort of painkiller

∗   *verb* **sorts, sorting, sorted**
If you sort things, you arrange them into classes or sets.
I'm sorting the library books.

➜   *phrase*
If you are **out of sorts**, you are not well.

sound[1] /**sound**/

∗   *adjective*

1   healthy
He's sound in mind and body.

2   strong
He has sound reasons for going.

3   without serious error or weakness
His work is quite sound.

sound

* *adverb*
completely
He was sound asleep.

sound² /sound/

* *noun* **sounds**
1 a noise
a strange sound
2 that which is heard
the speed of sound
* *verb* **sounds, sounding, sounded**
1 If something sounds, it makes a noise.
The car alarms were sounding.
2 If you sound something, you touch or hit it so
that it makes a noise.
They sounded the dinner bell.

south /south/

* *noun*
one of the main points of the compass, opposite
north
* *adjective*
being in the south, facing south
→ *word family*
southern /**suth**-ern/ *adjective*
relating to or from the south

space /space/

* *noun* **spaces**
1 (no plural) the whole extent of the universe not
occupied by solid bodies
The astronaut went into space.

2 the distance between one body or object and another
The spaces between the trees are each four metres long.

3 the place occupied by a person or thing
You're in my parking space.

4 a length of time
We've had two earthquakes in the space of a year.

* *verb* **spaces, spacing, spaced**
If you space things, you arrange them with gaps between them.
We've been spacing the new trees out across the field.

speak /**speek**/ *verb* **speak, speaking, spoke, spoken**
If you speak, you utter words or talk.
My daughter is learning to speak.

➔ *word family*
speaker /**spee**-ker/ *noun*
1 a person who speaks, especially in a particular way
a quiet speaker
2 the person in charge of a legislative assembly
the Speaker of the House of Commons

special /**spe**-shal/ *adjective*
1 having to do with one particular thing, person, or occasion
I have a special tool for the job.
2 not common or usual, distinctive
I've bought this for a special occasion.

➔ *word family*
specially /**spesh**-lee/ *adverb*
in a special manner

specialist /**spe**-shlist/ *noun*
a person who makes a particular study of one subject or of one branch of a subject
He is a cancer specialist.

speciality /spe-shee-**a**-li-tee/ *noun*

1 a particular field of work or study
Cosmetic surgery is his speciality.

2 something made or sold only by a certain place
Try the speciality of the house.

specialize /**spe**-sha-lize/ *verb* **specializes, specializing, specialized**
If you specialize in one subject, you make a particular study of it.
This doctor specializes in skin disorders.

speech /**speech**/ *noun* **speeches**

1 the ability to speak

2 a talk given in public
He gave a great speech at the wedding.

→ *word family*
speechless /**speech**-less/ *adjective*
unable to speak for love, surprise, fear, etc
I was speechless with rage.

speed /**speed**/

∗ *noun* **speeds**

1 quickness of movement
the speed of the car

2 haste
He moved with speed.

∗ *verb* **speed, speeding, sped** /**sped**/

1 If you speed, you go fast.
He was speeding down the road.

2 If you speed when you are driving a vehicle, you go faster than is allowed by law.

spend /spend/ *verb* **spends, spending, spent** /spent/
1 If you spend money, you pay it out.
I spent so much money last month.
➔ *collocation*
*He **spent** all of his money **on** books.*
2 If you spend something, you use it or use it up.
The soap is now spent.
3 If you spend time doing something, you do that thing, which is often something you like doing.
I have been spending a lot of time in the garden.
➔ *word family*
spender /spen-der/ *noun*
a person who spends money, especially someone who spends too much

staff /staff/
✳ *noun* **staffs**
1 any body of employees
the office staff
➔ *usage*
Remember that this sense of **staff** does not take a plural. It is always **staff**, never **staffs**.
2 a stick or rod used as a support
3 the set of five parallel lines on and between which musical notes are written.
✳ *verb* **staffs, staffing, staffed**
If you staff an organization, you provide it with workers or employees.
The office is staffed mainly by women.

stage /**stage**/

✳ *noun* **stages**
1 a raised platform for actors, performers, speakers, etc
2 the theatre
➔ *collocation*
   She is **on the stage.**
3 a certain point in development or progress
   There are several stages in the production
   process.
✳ *verb* **stages, staging, staged**
   If you stage a play, you get it performed publicly.
   We're staging a production of Hamlet.

stand /**stand**/

✳ *verb* **stands, standing, stood** /**stood**/
1 If you stand, you are upright on your feet and
   legs.
   The boys are standing over there.
2 If you stand up, you rise up.
   She stood up and left the room.
3 If you stand, you stop moving.
4 If something stands in a certain place, it is
   located there.
   A ruined house stood on the river bank.
5 If you can stand something, you can endure it.
   I can't stand loud music.
✳ *noun* **stands**
1 a small table, rack, etc, on which things may be
   placed or hung
2 a base or support on which an object may be
   placed upright
   I'm looking for a stand for the statue.

3 resistance
➔ *collocation*
You must try and **take a stand** against the
bully.
Take a stand against racism.
➔ *phrases*
If you **stand by** someone, you support them.
If you **stand down** from something, you withdraw
from it.
If you **stand fast**, you remain firm and determined.
If something **stands out**, it is prominent or
noticeable.

standard /**stan**-dard/
---
* *noun* **standards**
1 a fixed measure
2 an average level of accomplishment or quality
with which other work is compared
His work is below standard.
3 an upright post, etc, used for support
a door standard
* *adjective*
1 fixed
a standard letter
2 fixed by rule
➔ *word family*
standardize /**stan**-dar-dize/ *verb* **standardizes,**
standardizing, standardized
If you standardize things, you see that they are all
made or done in the same way.
We are thinking of standardizing the testing system.

start /start/

∗ *verb* **starts, starting, started**

1 If you start something, you begin it or set it in motion.
I'm about to start working.
He's starting a new business.

2 If you start at something, you jump or make a sudden movement in fright.
I started in alarm at the eerie sound.

∗ *noun* **starts**

1 a beginning
It's the start of the working day.

2 a sudden sharp movement
He gave a start at the noise.

station /stay-shun/

∗ *noun* **stations**

1 a regular stopping place for trains, buses, etc
a train station

2 a headquarters from which a public service is operated
fire station
police station

∗ *verb* **stations, stationing, stationed**
If you station someone in a place, you send them there to work.

stay /stay/

∗ *verb* **stays, staying, stayed**

1 If you stay in a certain state, you remain that way.

➜ *collocation*
*Please **stay calm**.*

2 If you stay in a place, you live there for a time.
I stayed in New York for a few years.

3 If you stay something, you delay it.
The judge decided to stay the execution.

* *noun* **stays**

1 time spent in a place
We had a lovely stay in the house.

2 a delay
There has already been one stay of execution for this prisoner.

step /step/
___

* *noun* **steps**

1 a pace taken by one foot

2 the distance covered by such a pace

3 a footprint
steps in the snow

4 the sound of a footfall
I heard steps on the stair.

5 a complete series of movements in a dance

6 one of a series of rungs or small graded platforms that allow a person to climb or walk from one level to another
The window cleaner climbed up the steps of his ladder.

* *verb* **steps, stepping, stepped**
If you step, you walk.
He stepped off the pavement.

➔ *phrases*
If you are **out of step,** you are behaving or thinking differently from others.
If you **step up** something, you increase it.
If you **take steps,** you take action.

still /still/

* *adjective* **stiller, stillest**
1 at rest, motionless
The water is very still.
2 calm, silent
a still night
* *noun* **stills**
a single photograph out of a series taken by a moving camera
* *verb* **stills, stilling, stilled**
If you still something, you make it calm, silent, or motionless.
* *adverb*
1 even so
Her father is old but still he wants to go on working.
2 up to this moment
They are still fighting.

stone /stone/

* *noun* **stones**
1 a hard mass of rock
2 a piece of rock, a pebble
3 the hard centre of some fruits
I took all the stones out of the cherries.
4 a piece of hard matter that forms in the body in certain diseases
kidney stones
5 a precious gem
a ring with many stones
6 in the imperial system, a unit of weight made up of 14 lbs
He was more than a stone overweight.

* *adjective*
made of stone

* *verb* **stones, stoning, stoned**

1 If you stone something, you throw stones at it.

2 If you stone fruit, you remove the stones from it.
He stoned the cherries.

➔ *idiom*
If you **leave no stone unturned**, you do everything possible in a situation.

---

stop /stop/

* *verb* **stops, stopping, stopped**

1 If you stop doing something, you no longer do it.
I have stopped smoking.

2 If you stop, you come to a standstill.

3 If you stop something up, you block or close it.
I tried to stop the hole in the pipe.

* *noun* **stops**

1 a pause
Suddenly there was a stop in the music.

2 a place where a bus, etc, halts to pick up passengers

➔ *word family*
stopper /stop-er/ *noun*
something that blocks up a small hole in something

---

story /stoe-ree/ *noun* **stories**

1 an account of events, real or imagined

➔ *collocation*
*Her mother read her a **bedtime story**.*

2 a lie
His account of the event was just a story.

straight /strate/

* *adjective* **straighter, straightest**
1 not curving or crooked
   a straight line
2 honest
   This company is totally straight.
* *adverb*
   directly, at once
   Come straight home after school.
→ ***word family***
   straighten /strate-en/ *verb*
   If you straighten something, you make it straight.
   I straighten the bedclothes every morning.

street /street/ *noun* **streets**

a public road lined with buildings in a city or town

strength /strength/ *noun* **strengths**

1 bodily power
   I don't have the strength to lift the load.
2 might, force
   the strength of the military
3 the number of people of a class, army, etc,
   present or on the roll
   Right now the staff is at full strength.
→ ***word family***
   strengthen /streng-then/ *verb*
   If you strengthen something, you make it stronger.
   The builder says we need to strengthen the roof.

strong /strong/ *adjective* **stronger, strongest**

1 powerful
   He has a strong influence on her sister.
2 healthy
   The children are getting strong after their illness.

3 possessing bodily power
He's a very strong man.

structure /**struc**-chur/ *noun* **structures**
1 a building
a wooden structure
2 anything consisting of parts put together
according to a plan
3 the way in which a thing is put together
→ *collocation*
*It's **part of the structure** of the organization.*
→ *word family*
structural /**struc**-chu-ral/ *adjective*
to do with the structure of something
a structural fault

student /**styoo**-dent/ *noun* **students**
a person who studies, a person who goes to
school
university students

studio /**styoo**-dee-o/ *noun* **studios**
1 the room in which a painter, sculptor,
photographer, etc, works
2 a building in which films are made
3 a place in which records are made or a room
from which radio or television programmes are
broadcast

study /**stu**-dee/
✳ *verb* **studies, studying, studied**
1 If you study something, you read about it to
obtain knowledge.
She studied history at university.

2 If you study something closely, you examine it.
The police are studying the evidence.

✳ *noun* **studies**
1 the obtaining of information, especially by reading
2 a subject studied
3 an office, a room set aside for reading and learning
The books are in my study.

➔ **word family**
studious /**styoo**-dee-us/ *adjective*
of, given to, or engaged in study
studious pupils

---

stuff /**stuff**/

✳ *noun*
1 the material or substance of which something is made
2 anything said, done, written, composed, etc
I prefer his older stuff to the new music.

➔ **usage**
Remember that you say **stuff** whether it is singular or plural, never **stuffs**.

✳ *verb* **stuffs, stuffing, stuffed**
If you stuff something, you fill it full or tightly.
He stuffed all his clothes into a suitcase.

➔ **word family**
stuffing /**stu**-fing/ *noun*
1 material used to stuff something hollow
I need to get some stuffing for cushions.
2 a mixture of breadcrumbs, seasoning, etc, put inside chickens, etc, when cooking
We're making chestnut stuffing for the turkey.

→ *usage*
Remember that you say **stuffing** whether it is singular or plural, never **stuffings**.

style /stile/ *noun* **styles**
1 manner of doing anything
→ *collocation*
*They don't like her **style of** teaching.*
2 a way of writing, painting, etc, by which works of art can be recognized as the work of a particular artist, school, or period
He discussed the style of the writer in an essay.
3 a fashion
the style of the 1920s
4 elegance
→ *collocation*
*She dresses **with style**.*
→ *word family*
stylish /stie-lish/ *adjective*
well dressed, smart, fashionable
stylist /stie-list/ *noun*
a person who designs, creates, or advises on current styles of clothing, hair, etc.

subject

∗ *adjective* /**sub**-jict/
1 ruled by
subject to the rules of international law
2 liable to
My son is subject to colds.
∗ *noun* /**sub**-jict/ **subjects**
1 a person who owes loyalty to a ruler or government

2   that about which something is said or written
He was the subject of the newspaper article.

3   something studied
She studied French among other subjects at school.

✳   *verb* /sub-**ject**/ **subjects, subjecting, subjected**
If you subject a person to something, you make them experience it.
He subjected them to ridicule.

such /**such**/

✳   *adjective*

1   of a like kind or degree, similar
I consider such behaviour to be unacceptable.

2   so extreme, so much, so great, etc
happy with such praise

✳   *adverb*
to so great a degree
This is such good news.

suggest /su-**jest**/ *verb* **suggests, suggesting, suggested**

1   If you suggest an idea, you put it forward to be considered.
I'm going to suggest some improvements.

2   If you suggest something to someone, you hint at it.

➔   *collocation*
*Are you **suggesting that** I am a liar?*

➔   *word family*
suggestion /su-**jes**-chun/ *noun*

1   a proposal
Can I make a suggestion?

2 a hint, slight indication
There was a suggestion that he had married her for her money.
suggestive /su-**jes**-tiv/ *adjective*
1 putting ideas into the mind
The book is suggestive of Victorian times.
2 rather indecent
He made suggestive remarks about her appearance.

sun /**sun**/ *noun* **suns**

1 (often **Sun**) the heavenly body that gives light and heat to the Earth and other planets in the same system
2 the warmth or light given by the sun

supply /su-**plie**/

✽ *verb* **supplies, supplying, supplied**
If you supply what is needed, you provide it.
We supplied food for the party.
✽ *noun* **supplies**
a steady amount of something that is needed
a supply of tea and coffee

support /su-**poart**/ *verb* **supports, supporting, supported**

1 If you support something, you help to hold it up.
The struts supported the bridge.
2 If you support a cause, you give help or encouragement to it.
They support the campaign for independence.

3 If you support someone, you provide them with the necessities of life.
She's the only one who financially supports her family.

4 If you provide someone with support, you help or encourage them.
She supported me through that tough time.

→ *word family*
supportive /su-**poar**-tiv/ *adjective*
used to describe someone who or something that supports
supporter /su-**poar**-ter/ *noun*
a person who helps or encourages
They are supporters of the president's cause.

suppose /su-**poaz**/ *verb* **supposes, supposing, supposed**

1 If you suppose something, you believe it to be true without sure evidence.
We suppose that he is honest.

2 If you suppose, you imagine.
I suppose she has gone home.

→ *word family*
supposed /su-**poe**-zid, su-**pozed**/ *adjective*

1 believed or imagined
That was his supposed meaning.

2 intended or designed
What was he supposed to do?

3 meant, allowed
The children aren't supposed to talk during class.
supposedly /su-**poe**-zid-lee/ *adverb*
according to what is, was, or may be supposed
We are supposedly having a meeting about this.

sure /**shoor**/ *adjective* **surer, surest**

1   certain
    I'm sure he'll come.
2   convinced of
    She is sure of her own ability.
3   unfailing
    This is a sure remedy.

surface /**sur**-fiss/

*   *noun* **surfaces**
1   the outside or top part of anything
2   outside appearance
    She seems happy on the surface but I know that inside she is really unhappy.

*   *verb* **surfaces, surfacing, surfaced**
    If you surface from water, you rise up to the surface from down below.
    It seemed ages before she surfaced.

system /**si**-stum/ *noun* **systems**

1   a method by which a number of parts of different kinds are made to work together as a whole
→   *collocations*
    the **nervous system**
    a **transport system**
    the **solar system**
2   a regular method of doing things
→   *collocation*
    He has **no system of** working.
3   a plan
→   *collocation*
    He has a **system for** winning the lottery.

table

→ **word family**
systematic /si-stu-**mat**-ic/ *adjective*
methodical, arranged in an orderly or reasonable
manner
systematize /**si**–stu-ma-tize/ *verb* **systematizes,**
systematizing, systematized
If you systematize something, you give it a
system.

table /**tay**-bul/

* *noun* **tables**
1   an article of furniture with legs and a flat top,
    used for placing or resting things on
    Can you put that on the dining table?
2   a list of figures, names, facts, etc, arranged in
    columns
    The table is showing the times of the buses.
* *verb* **tables, tabling, tabled**
    If you table a discussion, you put it forward.
→ **collocation**
    *We're **tabling a motion**.*
→ **idiom**
    If you **turn the tables on** someone, you begin
    doing to them what they have been doing to you.

take /take/ *verb* **takes, taking, took, taken**

1   If you take something, you seize or grasp it.
2   If you take something from someone, you receive
    or accept it.
3   If you take something or someone, you capture it
    or them.
    The army took the city.

4 If you take something somewhere, you carry it with you to that place.

5 If you take the bus or train, you travel by it.

➔ *phrases*

If you **take after** someone, you are like them.

If you **take something down**, you write notes, etc.

If you **take heart**, you become braver.

If you **take someone in**, you deceive them.

If you **take something off**, you remove it.

If you **take someone on**, you agree to play or fight against them.

If you **take something over**, you get control of it.

---

talk /tawk/
_____

✱ *verb* **talks, talking, talked**

If you talk, you speak words.

✱ *noun* **talks**

1 a conversation

I had an interesting talk with them.

2 a lecture

He gave a talk on local history.

3 gossip

There is a lot of talk about their affair.

➔ *phrases*

If you **talk something over**, you discuss it.

If you **talk someone round**, you convince them to do something they did not want to do at first.

➔ *word family*

talkative /**taw**-ka-tiv/ *adjective*

fond of talking

tea /**tee**/ *noun* **teas**

1   a shrub found in India and China
2   its dried leaves
3   a drink made by pouring boiling water on dried
    tea leaves
    I would like a cup of tea.
4   a light afternoon or evening meal
    I'd like to invite them to tea.

team /**teem**/ *noun* **teams**

1   a number of people working together for the
    same purpose
    There is a team of people working on the project.
2   a set of players on one side in a game
    a football team
➜   *word family*
    teamwork /**teem**-wurk/ *noun*
    united effort for the common good or a shared goal

technology /tek-**nol**-o-jee/ *noun* **technologies**

1   the application of science, especially to industrial
    or commercial objectives
2   the methods, theory, and practices governing
    such application
    a highly developed technology
➜   *word family*
    technological /tek-nu-**lodge**-ic-al/ *adjective*
    to do with technology
    technological progress

tell /**tell**/ *verb* **tells, telling, told** /**toald**/

    If you tell someone something, you say it, or give
    them an account of it.

➔ *word family*
telling /**te**-ling/ *adjective*
very effective or informative
It was a telling remark.

term /**term**/ *noun* **terms**
1 a limited period of time
   It happened during the term of the contract.
2 a word or phrase used in a particular study
   This is a technical term.
3 a division of the school year
   the summer term
➔ *phrases*
   If you **come to terms**, you make an agreement.
   If you **come to terms with** something, you come to accept it.
   If you are **on good terms with** someone, you are friendly.

test /**test**/
* *noun* **tests**
   an examination or trial intended to reveal quality, ability, progress, etc
* *verb* **tests, testing, tested**
1 If you test something, you try the quality or endurance of it.
   Let's test the new car.
2 If you test someone, you examine their knowledge of or ability in a subject.
   The teacher tested his French.
➔ *word family*
   testing /**tess**-ting/ *adjective*

If something is testing, it requires all your ability and effort to accomplish it.

These are testing times.

testy /**tess**-tee/ *adjective*
irritable

---

text /**tekst**/

* *noun* **texts**
1 the words actually written by the author not including notes, drawings, etc
2 a short passage from the Bible
3 subject, topic
the text of his speech
4 a text message
She sent me a text about the plans for the weekend.

* *verb* **texts, texting, texted**
If you text someone, you send a text message to them.

→ *word family*
textbook /**tekst**-book/ *noun*
a book about a subject written for those studying it
a maths textbook
text message /**tekst meh**-sidge/ *noun*
a message typed into a mobile phone and sent to another mobile phone

---

textile /**tek**-stile/ *noun* **textiles**
a fabric made by weaving

---

than /**than**/ *conjunction*
compared with
Jack is older than Kristina.

thank /thangk/

---

* *verb* **thanks, thanking, thanked**

If you thank someone, you show your gratitude.

He thanked the man warmly for saving his dog's life.

→ *collocation*

If someone or something is **to thank for something** they are responsible for it.

*He has his wife **to thank for** getting him that loan.*

→ *word family*

thankful /**thangk**-ful/ *adjective*

appreciative

We're thankful that the accident was not worse.

thankfully /**thangk**-fu-lee/ *adverb*

fortunately

Thankfully I do not have to work on Saturdays any more.

thank goodness /thangk **good**-ness/ *interjection, sentence substitute.*

The ordeal is over. Thank goodness!

thankless /**thangk**-less/ *adjective*

If something is not appreciated, it is thankless.

→ *phrases*

*Cleaning that kitchen was **a thankless task**.*

thanks /thangks/ *interjection, sentence substitute*

Thanks, I could not have done that on my own.

* *plural noun*

the expression of your gratitude

He gave thanks for the lovely meal.

→ *collocation*

***Thanks to** Harry I have no chocolate left.*

thank you /**thangk**-you/

* *interjection*

an expression of gratitude

Thank you so much for your help.

Thank you! You've made my day with that joke.

* *noun*

A big thank you to Bob for his efforts.

that /**that**/

* *adjective* **those** /**thoaz**/

being the person or thing there

that man with the black hair

That is my house over there.

* *pronoun*

who or which

This is the dress that I bought in New York.

* *conjunction*

introduces a statement, a wish, etc

He said that he was hungry.

the /**thi**/, /**thee**/ *definite article*

referring to a particular person or thing

the woman in the black hat

their /**thayr**/, **theirs** /**thayrz**/ *possessive pronoun*

belonging to them

This cat is theirs.

then /**then**/ *adverb*

1 at that time

I was living in America then.

2 after that

I got up and then I got dressed.

3 therefore
If the party is on Saturday then I will be able to come.

---

there /**thare**/ *adverb*

in that place
Put your coat over there.

---

they /**thay**/ *pronoun*

the people or things already mentioned
While the boys were playing they lost their ball.

---

thing /**thing**/ *noun* **things**

1 any single existing object
There are a lot of things in that cupboard.
2 whatever may be thought of or spoken about
I'm worried about this court thing.
3 a happening
Are you going to this thing on Monday?
4 Your things are your possessions.
Leave my things alone!

---

think /**thingk**/ *verb* **thinks, thinking, thought** /**thot**/

1 If you think, you form ideas in the mind.
I've had no time to think.
2 If you think something, you believe it.
He thinks it is wrong.

→ *word family*
thinker /**thing**-ker/ *noun*
a person who thinks
thinking /**thing**-king/ *adjective*
able to think or reason

this /**this**/ *adjective, pronoun* **these** /**theez**/

being the person or thing here
This painting is the one that was damaged.
These are my sisters.

though /**thoa**/ *preposition*

despite the fact that
I will be there, though I would rather not.

thought /**thawt**/

* *past tense of* **think**
  I thought you had already left.
* *noun* **thoughts**
1 the power or act of thinking
2 what you think, an idea
   I had a sad thought.
→ *word family*
   thoughtful /**thawt**-ful/ *adjective*
1 given to thinking
2 considerate, thinking of others
   a thoughtful gift
   thoughtless /**thawt**-less/ *adjective*
1 not thinking before acting
2 inconsiderate, not thinking of others
   a thoughtless remark

title /**tie**-tul/ *noun* **titles**

1 the name of a book, piece of writing or music,
   picture, etc
2 a name or word used in addressing someone, to
   indicate rank, office, etc
3 a claim to ownership, a right

to /**too**/ preposition

used to show movement towards
I'm driving to school tomorrow.

today /to-**day**/

* *noun*

the present day
Today is Monday.

* *adverb*

1 on this day
I'm going to the dentist today.
2 nowadays, at the present time
Children have no manners today.
Today, it's a thriving city.

together /to-**ge**-ther/ adverb

with another or others, in company
Let's all go together.

tomorrow /to-**mor**-ow/

* *noun*

the day after today
Tomorrow is Sunday.

* *adverb*

on the day after today
I'll be away tomorrow.

too /**too**/ adverb

1 also
Steve is hungry and I am too.
2 excessively
I'm too young to get married.

top /top/

* *noun* **tops**
1   the highest part or place
    I climbed to the top of the tree.
2   the summit
    We walked to the top of the mountain.
3   a garment worn on the upper body, such as a
    sweater or a T-shirt
* *adjective*
1   highest
    the top floor
2   most important
    the top job in the company
* *verb* **tops, topping, topped**
    If you top something, you are at the top of it.
    It was several hours before we finally topped the mountain.

total /**toe**-tal/

* *adjective*
1   whole
    the total cost
2   complete
    The car was a total wreck.
* *noun* **totals**
1   the whole amount
    I'll pay the total.
2   the result when everything has been added up
    The total comes to just over a hundred pounds.
* *verb* **totals, totalling, totalled**
1   If you total something, you add it up.
    I was asked to total the items on the bill.
2   If something totals something, it adds up to it.
    Sales this year will total one million dollars.

→ **word family**
totally /**toe**-ta-lee/ *adverb*
completely
totally wet

---

touch /**tuch**/
---
* *verb* **touches, touching, touched**
1 If you touch something, you come to rest it
against any part of the body, especially the
hand.
I touched her face with my hand.
2 If something touches you, it causes you to feel
emotion.
→ **collocation**
*I was really very **touched by** the poem.*
* *noun*
1 act of coming against or being in contact with
2 the ability to do something really well
→ **phrase**
*She **has a magic touch** with children.*
3 the sense of feeling
→ **phrase**
If you are **in touch** with someone, you are in
contact with them.
*We are no longer **in touch**.*
→ **word family**
touching /**tu**-ching/ *adjective*
moving the feelings, causing pity

---

towards /too-**ordz**/ *preposition*
---
in the direction of
I moved towards the door.

town /taoon/ noun towns

a group of houses, shops, etc, larger than a village but smaller than a city

trade /trade/

* *noun* **trades**
1 the buying and selling of goods
2 the exchanging of goods
* *verb* **trades, trading, traded**
1 If you trade, you buy and sell things.
2 If you trade things, you exchange them.
The children trade lunch every day.

train /train/

* *verb* **trains, training, trained**
1 If you train someone, you prepare them for something by constant practice or teaching.
I was training the basketball team.
2 If you train a plant, you make it to grow in a particular direction.
I was trying to train the vine along the wall.
* *noun* **trains**
1 railway carriages drawn by an engine
2 part of a dress that trails behind the wearer
The bride's train was five feet long.
3 a series
I interrupted her train of thought.
➔ *word family*
trainee /tray-**nee**/ *noun*
someone who trains for something, especially a job

trouble /**tru**-bl/

* *verb* **troubles, troubling, troubled**

1 If something troubles you, it causes you anxiety, difficulty, or distress.
His daughter's absence troubled him.

2 If you are troubled by something, you are disturbed by it.
I am sorry to trouble you.

* *noun* **troubles**

1 worry, anxiety, distress
Her son causes her a lot of trouble.

2 difficulty
I am having trouble closing the door.

➜ *word family*
troublesome /**tru**-bl-sum/ *adjective*
causing trouble
It's a troublesome task.

truth /**trooth**/ *noun*

that which is true
Always tell the truth.

➜ *word family*
truthful /**trooth**-ful/ *adjective*
honest
a truthful answer
truthfully /**trooth**-ful-ee/ *adverb*
honestly
I tried to answer truthfully.

try /**trie**/ *verb* **tries, trying, tried**

1 If you try to do something, you attempt to do it.
I tried to climb the tree.

2 If you try something, you test it or experience it for the first time.

Have you tried the new restaurant in town?

3 If someone is tried for something, they are examined and judged in a court of law.

He was tried for murder but found innocent.

→ **word family**

trying /**trie**-ing/ *adjective*

difficult, worrying, annoying

It has been a trying time for everyone.

---

turn /**turn**/

---

* *verb* **turns, turning, turned**

1 If someone or something turns, they or it move or are caused to move around.

She turned to face him.

2 If someone turns into something, they change.

→ *collocation*

*She has **turned into** a beautiful young woman.*

* *noun* **turns**

1 a change of direction.

They made a right turn at the crossroads.

2 a revolution of a wheel, or a round thing

Give the dial one turn to the left.

3 a bend

The accident happened at the turn in the road.

4 an act

She did him a good turn.

5 a short walk

The old couple took a turn along the promenade.

6 an opportunity to do something that multiple people are wanting or waiting to do

She wants a turn on the swing.

➔ **phrases**

If you **turn something down**, you refuse it.

If you **turn in**, you go to bed.

If you **turn out**, you attend a meeting.

If you **turn up**, you appear unexpectedly.

If you **turn upon** or **turn on** someone, you attack them suddenly.

➔ **idiom**

If you **turn over a new leaf**, you change yourself for the better.

two /**too**/ noun

the number 2, coming between one and three

type /**tipe**/

∗ noun **types**

1 a class or kind
   Spinach is a type of vegetable.

2 a person or thing possessing most of the qualities of a certain group, nationality, etc

3 a letter or symbol cut in metal, etc, and used for printing

∗ verb **types, typing, typed**

If you type, you use a keyboard to write.

➔ **collocation**

*He is **typing a letter.***

unable /u-**nay**-bul/ adjective

not able, lacking the ability, means, or power to do something

under /**un**-der/

∗ preposition

1 below
   under a tree

2 subject to
under military law
* *adverb*
in or to a lower condition, degree, or place
He stood at the edge of the pool and then dived under.

understand /un-der-**stand**/ *verb* **understands,
understanding, understood**

1 If you understand something, you see the
meaning of it.
I don't understand the poem.
2 If you understand someone or something, you
know them or it thoroughly.
*It took her some time to understand the filing
system.*
3 If you understand the truth, you work it out from
what has been said.
I think I understand his motives.
→ *word family*
understanding /un-der-**stan**-ding/ *noun*
1 intelligence, powers of judgment
2 an agreement, especially an unwritten one
*There was an understanding that the money would
be paid every month.*

unit /**yoo**-nit/ *noun* **units**

1 the number one
2 a single person, thing, or group
a military unit
3 a fixed amount, etc, taken as a standard in
measuring
metric units

university /yoo-ni-**ver**-si-tee/ *noun* **universities**

a place of higher education in which advanced study in all branches of knowledge is carried on, and by which degrees are awarded

unless /un-**less**/ *conjunction*

if not, except that
Don't make a promise unless you can keep it.

until /un-**til**/

✱ *preposition*
up to the time of
I lived with my parents until last year.

✱ *conjunction*
up to the time when
I waited until she had left the room.

unusual /un-**yoozh**-wal/ *adjective*

rare, peculiar, strange
unusual birds

up /**up**/

✱ *adverb*
in or to a higher place, amount, etc
Lift me up.
Prices have gone up.

✱ *preposition*
to, toward, or at a higher place on or in
We climbed up the hill.

upon /up-**on**/ *adverb*

on, used only for completing a verb
We need to decide upon a name for the baby.

upper /**up**-er/

* *adjective*
  higher in place or rank
  an upper floor
* *noun* **uppers**
  the part of a shoe that is above the sole

upset

* *verb* /up-**set**/ **upsets, upsetting, upset**
1   If you are upset by something, it causes you to be
    sad, worried, etc.
    His remarks greatly upset her.
2   If you upset something, you overturn or knock it over.
    The tables were upset during the fight.
3   If something is upset, it is spoiled completely.
    Our plans were upset because of a change in the weather.
* *adjective* /up-**set**/
1   worried, disturbed
    I am upset about the quarrel.
2   ill, physically unwell
    an upset stomach
* *noun* /**up**-set/ **upsets**
1   disturbance of the emotions
    the upset caused by his sudden death
2   trouble
    There was an upset at work today.
3   a stomach upset is a slight illness in your
    stomach

urban /**ur**-ban/ *adjective*

having to do with a city or city life
urban regeneration

us /**us**/ *pronoun*

the writer or speaker together with another person or other people
Tell us your news.

use

* *verb* /**yooz**/ **uses, using, used**
1 If you use something, you employ it or do something with it for a purpose.
Use a knife to cut the butter.
She uses a great many long words.
* *noun* /**yooss**/ **uses**
1 the act of using, the state of being used
This is only for use in emergencies.
2 advantage, benefit, value
This book is of no use to us.
3 the power of using
She has lost the use of her legs.
4 permission to use, the right to use
Give them the use of the car.
→ *phrase*
If you **use something up**, you consume or exhaust it, leaving nothing.

usual /**yoo**-zh-wal/ *adjective*

common, normal
It's the usual price.

value /**val**-yoo/ *noun* **values**

1 worth, importance
information that was of value to the police
2 price, cost
the market value of the vase

3 (**values**) the standards by which you judge the worth of things
moral values
➔ *word family*
valuer /**val**-yoo-er/ *noun*
a person who estimates the value of things
valuable /**val**-yoo-bl/ *adjective*
of great value

vehicle /**vee**-i-cul/ *noun*

1 any type of car, carriage, train, bus, etc, used on land for carrying people or things
motor vehicles
2 a means of doing something
The internet is a vehicle of communication.
➔ *word family*
vehicular /vee-**hi**-cyu-lar/ *adjective*
to do with vehicles
vehicular traffic

very /**ve**-ree/

✳ *adverb*
extremely
It's very hot today.
a very beautiful child
✳ *adjective*
true, real, exact
He's the very person we were looking for.

view /**vyoo**/

✳ *noun* **views**
1 all that can be seen at one look or from one point, a scene
The view from the hill is spectacular.

2 opinion
In his view she is not suitable for the job.
3 intention
We bought the house with the view to divide it into flats.
✳ *verb* **views, viewing, viewed**
1 If you view something, you look at it.
I would like to view the property.
2 If you view something, you examine or consider it.
We are viewing all possible solutions.
➔ *word family*
viewer /**vyoo**-wer/ *noun*
a person who watches something
television viewers

---

village /**vi**-lidge/ *noun* **villages**

a group of houses, shops, etc, smaller than a town
➔ *word family*
villager /**vi**-li-jer/ *noun*
a person who lives in a village

---

visit /**vi**-zit/

✳ *verb* **visits, visiting, visited**
If you visit someone, you go to see or stay with them.
He's visiting his parents.
✳ *noun* **visits**
1 a call upon
a hospital visit
2 a short stay
a visit to the seaside
➔ *word family*
visitor /**vi**-zi-tur/ *noun*
a person who visits

vital /**vie**-tal/ *adjective*

1 very important
   The meeting was vital to the peace treaty.

2 unable to be done without, necessary to life
   These are vital organs.

➔ ***word family***
   vitally /**vie**-ta-lee/ *adverb*
   importantly

voice /**voiss**/

∗ *noun* **voices**

1 the sound produced through the mouth when
   speaking or singing
   The choir boy has a lovely voice.

2 a vote, an opinion
   the voice of the people

3 the right to speak or express an opinion
   The workers had no voice.

∗ *verb* **voices, voicing, voiced**
   If you voice something, you say or express it.
   They voiced their disapproval.

➔ ***word family***
   voicemail /**voiss**-male/ *noun*
   an electronic system for storing telephone
   messages so that they can be listened to later

volume /**vol**-yoom/ *noun* **volumes**

1 a book
   a dusty volume

2 one of a series in a set of books
   volume three of the encyclopedia

3 the amount of space taken up by anything
   the volume of water in the tank

4 a large mass or amount
the volume of trade

5 level of sound
Turn up the volume on the radio.

---

want /**wawnt**/

✱ *noun* **wants**

1 need
people in want of food

2 longing
a want for peace and quiet

3 shortage
a want of shelter and warm clothes

✱ *verb* **wants**, **wanting, wanted**

1 If you want something, or want for something, you lack it or need it.
He wants for food.
Those windows want cleaning.

2 If you want someone or something, you desire them or it.
I want a new bike.
I want to get out of here right now.

➜ *phrase*
If you **want for nothing** you have everything you need.
You will want for nothing if you join that company.

➜ *word family*
wanting /**wawn**-ting/ *adjective*

1 not as good as required

➜ *collocation*
*She **found** his work **wanting**.*

2 lacking
The door is wanting a handle.

water /**waw**-ter/

✱ *noun* **waters**

1 the clear liquid that falls as rain and flows in streams and rivers

2 a large area of water, as a lake, sea, etc
stormy waters

✱ *verb* **waters, watering, watered**

1 If you water something, you supply it with water.
You must feed and water the horses before you go.

2 If you water a garden or plants, you pour or sprinkle water on it or them.

way /**way**/ *noun* **ways**

1 a track, path, or road
the way through the woods

2 a method of doing something
a new way of teaching

3 distance travelled
It is a long way to the next village.

4 the route to a place
the way to the station

5 a custom or habit
He has a way of upsetting people.

➔ *idioms*
If you **have a way with** something, you have such a manner or skill as to handle it successfully.
If something is **under way**, it is in movement or process.
If you have **ways and means**, you have methods of doing things.

we /**wee**/ *pronoun*

refers to the speaker or writer and another person or other people
We all went to church.

week /**week**/ *noun* **weeks**
>a period of seven days

well¹ /**well**/
* *adverb* **better, best**
1   in a good way or style
>*She does her job well.*
2   thoroughly
>*Examine the house well before buying it.*
3   rightly
>*You may well apologize.*
4   with approval
>*She speaks well of him.*
* *adjective*
>in good health
>*I haven't been well.*
→ *phrase*
>The phrase **as well as** means in addition to.
>*I brought coffee as well as tea.*

well² /**well**/
* *noun* **wells**
>a spring of water or a hole in the ground from which water can be drawn
* *verb* **wells, welling, welled**
>If something wells, it comes up as from a spring or gushes out.
>*Tears were welling from her eyes.*

which /**which**/
* *adjective*
>what particular
>*Which picture do you prefer?*

while

* *pronoun*
  what particular person or thing
  Which is your house?

while /while/

* *conjunction*
  during the time that
  While we were inside, someone stole our car.
* *noun*
  a space of time
  It's a while since I saw you.
* *verb* **whiles, whiling, whiled**
→ *phrase*
  If you **while away** time, you pass it in pleasure or leisure.
  He whiled away the afternoon reading.

white /white/

* *adjective* **whiter, whitest**
1 of the colour of clean snow or milk
   I saw a white cat in a tree.
2 pale
   Her illness has made her look rather white.
3 having a pale skin
   People with fair skin need to be careful in the sun.
* *noun*
  the colour white
  White is the best colour to paint a small room.

whole /hole/

* *adjective*
1 complete, entire
   I'm tired of the whole affair.

2   unharmed
    He managed to escape whole from the accident.

✱   *noun*
    the total, all
    I ate the whole of the cake myself.

whose /**hooz**/ *pronoun*

belonging to whom
Whose is this sweater?

why /**whie**/ *adverb*

for what reason
Why are you here?

wife /**wife**/ *noun* **wives** /**waeevz**/

a married woman

will¹ /**will**/ *verb* **would** /**wood**/

If you say you will do something, you intend to do
it in the future.
I will be over to see you this evening.

will² /**will**/

✱   *noun* **wills**
1   your power to make decisions or choices, self-control
    I believe in freedom of the will.
2   desire
    It was done against her will.
3   a written document made by a person to say what
    is to be done with their property after death
✱   *verb* **wills, willing, willed**
1   If you will something to happen, you desire it to
    happen.
    We are willing her to win.

2 If you will something to someone, you leave it to them in your will (sense **3** above).

→ *word family*
wilful /**wil**-ful/ *adjective*

1 always wanting your own way
a wilful child

2 done deliberately
wilful destruction

---

within /wi-**thin**/ *preposition*

1 inside
The key is within the box.

2 before some time has passed
I hope to have the book finished within the week.

3 not beyond the limits of
to live within your means

---

without /wi-**thout**/ *preposition*

not having
without a coat
without money

---

woman /**woo**-man/ *noun* **women** /**wi**-men/

a grown-up female human being

→ *word family*
womanhood /**woo**-man-hood/ *noun*
the state or qualities of a woman
womankind /woo-man-**kiend**/ or **womenfolk** /**wi**-min-foke/ *plural noun*
women in general
womanly /**woo**-man-lee/ *adjective*
having the qualities of a woman

word /**wurd**/ *noun* **words**

1   a sound or group of sounds expressing an idea
2   a message, information
    Send him word about the accident.
3   a promise
    He gave his word that he would be there.

→ *idioms*
    If you **have words with** someone, you quarrel with them.
    If you say something **word for word**, you say it in exactly the same way as before.

→ *word family*
    wording /**wur**-ding/ *noun*
    the way that something is expressed in words
    The wording was difficult to understand.

work /**wurk**/

*   *noun*
1   effort
    He put a lot of work into the project.
2   a task, tasks
    I tend to bring work home from the office.
3   that which you do for a living
    He is at work seven hours a day.

*   **works** *plural noun*
1   a factory
    a print works
2   the parts of a machine that make it go

*   *verb* **works, working, worked**
1   If you work at a job, you are in that job.

→ *collocation*
    *I **work as** a teacher.*

2 If you work, you labour or toil.

→ *collocation*

They really **worked at** getting the house ready.

3 If you work someone, you make them do work.

He worked his employees hard.

4 If something works, it has the desired effect or result.

The painkillers did not work.

→ *phrase*

If you **work someone up**, you excite them.

→ *word family*

workable /**wur**-ka-bul/ *adjective*

that can be done or used

It's a workable plan.

worker /**wur**-ker/ *noun*

1 a person who works

the factory workers

2 an insect such as a bee that does all the work

workforce /**wurk**-foarss/ *noun*

the number of people who work in a particular firm, place, industry, etc

---

world /**wurld**/ *noun* **worlds**

1 the Earth on which we live

2 any planet or star

3 the universe and all things

4 all human beings

5 any sphere of activity, study, etc

→ *collocation*

the **world of** science

→ *word family*

worldly /**wurld**-lee/ *adjective*

1 having to do with this world or life

worldly wisdom

2 interested only in the things of this life
worldly people

---

worth /**wurth**/

✱ *adjective*
1 equal in value to
The gold bracelet was worth a lot of money.
2 deserving of
It's a film worth seeing.
3 having a particular amount of money or property
He's worth millions.
✱ *noun*
1 value
The painting's worth is incalculable.
2 price
Thousands of pounds' worth of jewellery was stolen in the robbery.
3 merit, excellence
He proved his worth by going.

➜ *word family*
worthless /**wurth**-less/ *adjective*
of no use or value
worthlessness /**wurth**-less-ness/ *noun*
the state of having no use or value
worthwhile /wurth-**while**/ *adjective*
profitable, repaying the money, work, etc,
expended
He does a worthwhile job.
worthy /**wur**-thee/ *adjective*
deserving, deserving respect
a worthy cause

wrong /rong/

* *adjective*
1 not correct, false
   the wrong answer
2 incorrect in your opinion, etc
   I think it's the wrong decision.
3 not good, not morally right, evil
   Murder is wrong.

* *verb* **wrongs, wronging, wronged**
   If you wrong someone, you treat them unjustly or harm them.
   I was wronged by my previous employer.

* *noun*
   an injustice
   A terrible wrong has been done to him.

→ *word family*
   wrongly /**rong**-li/ *adverb*
   badly, incorrectly
   wrongly imprisoned
   wrongdoer /**rong**-doo-er/ *noun*
   a criminal, a sinner
   wrongdoing /**rong**-doo-ing/ *noun*
   something which is wrong
   wrongful /**rong**-ful/ *adjective*
   unjust, illegal, immoral
   wrongful arrest

year /yeer/ *noun* **years**

1 the time taken by the Earth to travel once around the sun
2 365 days, especially from 1 January to 31 December, 12 months

yes /**yes**/ *sentence substitute*

used to express consent, agreement, approval, etc

you /**yoo**/ *pronoun*

the person or people who you are addressing, in speech or writing

You were in my maths class at school, remember?

You must then whisk the egg whites till very stiff.

I'd like you all to turn to page thirteen.

➜ *word family*

your *determiner*

belonging to the person being addressed

I like your coat.

you're *contraction of* **you are**

You're coming with me.

yours *pronoun*

refers to a thing that belongs to the person being addressed.

This coat is mine and this is yours.

yourself *reflexive pronoun* **yourselves**

You should think of yourself at this difficult time.

yours truly *pronoun*

another way of saying **I, myself, me**; an informal and humorous way of referring to yourself

➜ *phrase*

You would say **you know what?** to introduce and emphasize a statement.

You know what? I'm tired of your excuses.

You know what? I've had the time of my life!

→ *usage*
You is the correct singular and plural usage. You do not refer to a group of people as **yous**.

young /**yung**/
* *adjective* **younger, youngest**
not old, not grown up, childish, youthful
a young child
a young attitude
* *noun*
1 all the children or offspring of
the lioness and her young
2 young people in general
→ *collocation*
This film is definitely for **the young**.
→ *usage*
Remember that the word **young** does not take a plural.

zero /**zee**-ro/ *noun* **zeros or zeroes**
1 the figure 0
2 the 0-mark on a measuring scale
3 (informal) worthless, without any importance
He went from hero to zero.

GRAMMAR HELP

COMMON IRREGULAR VERBS

infinitive	simple past	past participle
be	was, were	been
bear	bore	born
beat	beat	beaten
become	became	become
begin	began	begun
bend	bent	bent
bet	bet	bet
bid	bid	bid
bind	bound	bound
bite	bit	bitten
bleed	bled	bled
blow	blew	blown
break	broke	broken
breed	bred	bred
bring	brought	brought
broadcast	broadcast	broadcast
browbeat	browbeat	browbeaten
build	built	built
burn	burned / burnt	burned / burnt
burst	burst	burst
bust	busted / bust	busted / bust
buy	bought	bought
cast	cast	cast
catch	caught	caught
choose	chose	chosen
cling	clung	clung
clothe	clothed	clothed / clad
come	came	come
cost	cost	cost
creep	crept	crept

infinitive	simple past	past participle
cut	cut	cut
deal	dealt	dealt
dig	dug	dug
disprove	disproved	disproved / disproven
dive	dived / dove	dived
do	did	done
draw	drew	drawn
dream	dreamed / dreamt	dreamed / dreamt
drink	drank	drunk
drive	drove	driven
dwell	dwelled / dwelt	dwelled / dwelt
eat	ate	eaten
fall	fell	fallen
feed	fed	fed
feel	felt	felt
fight	fought	fought
find	found	found
flee	fled	fled
fling	flung	flung
fly	flew	flown
forbid	forbade	forbidden
forecast	forecast	forecast
forget	forgot	forgotten
forgive	forgave	forgiven
freeze	froze	frozen
get	got	got
give	gave	given
go	went	gone
grind	ground	ground
grow	grew	grown
hang	hung	hung
have	had	had
hear	heard	heard

infinitive	simple past	past participle
hide	hid	hidden
hit	hit	hit
hold	held	held
hurt	hurt	hurt
keep	kept	kept
kneel	kneeled / knelt	kneeled /knelt
knit	knitted	knitted
know	knew	known
lay	laid	laid
lead	led	led
lean	leaned / leant	leaned / leant
leap	leaped / leapt	leaped / leapt
learn	learned / learnt	learned / learnt
leave	left	left
lend	lent	lent
let	let	let
lie	lay	lain
light	lit / lighted	lit / lighted
lose	lost	lost
make	made	made
mean	meant	meant
meet	met	met
mistake	mistook	mistaken
misunderstand	misunderstood	misunderstood
offset	offset	offset
pay	paid	paid
prove	proved	proven / proved
put	put	put
quit	quit	quit
read	read	read
rid	rid	rid
ride	rode	ridden
ring	rang	rung

Grammar Help

infinitive	simple past	past participle
rise	rose	risen
run	ran	run
say	said	said
see	saw	seen
seek	sought	sought
sell	sold	sold
send	sent	sent
set	set	set
shake	shook	shaken
shine	shined / shone	shined / shone
shoot	shot	shot
show	showed	shown / showed
shrink	shrank / shrunk	shrunk
shut	shut	shut
sight-read	sight-read	sight-read
sing	sang	sung
sink	sank / sunk	sunk
sit	sat	sat
sleep	slept	slept
smell	smelled / smelt	smelled / smelt
speak	spoke	spoken
speed	sped / speeded	sped / speeded
spend	spent	spent
spill	spilled / spilt	spilled / spilt
spin	spun	spun
split	split	split
spoil	spoiled / spoilt	spoiled / spoilt
spring	sprang / sprung	sprung
stand	stood	stood
steal	stole	stolen
stick	stuck	stuck
sting	stung	stung
stink	stunk / stank	stunk

infinitive	simple past	past participle
strew	strewed	strewn / strewed
stride	strode	stridden
string	strung	strung
strive	strove / strived	striven / strived
swear	swore	sworn
swell	swelled	swollen
swim	swam	swum
swing	swung	swung
take	took	taken
teach	taught	taught
tear	tore	torn
tell	told	told
think	thought	thought
throw	threw	thrown
thrust	thrust	thrust
upset	upset	upset
wake	woke / waked	woken / waked
wear	wore	worn
weave	wove / weaved	woven / weaved
wed	wed / wedded	wed / wedded
weep	wept	wept
wet	wet	wet / wetted
win	won	won
wind	wound	wound
withdraw	withdrew	withdrawn
withhold	withheld	withheld
write	wrote	written

Grammar Help

ARTICLES

indefinite: a/an
definite: the

MODAL VERBS

can   shall
could   should
may   will
might   would
must

PRONOUNS

subject	object	possessive
I	me	mine
you	you	yours
he	him	his
she	her	hers
it	it	its
we	us	ours
you	you	yours
they	them	theirs

my

verb   *noun*

my wife

PREPOSITIONS, CONJUNCTIONS AND ADVERBS

above
according to
after
against
already
always
and
at
at once
at times
backwards
badly
because
before
behind
between
but
close to
down
during
either ... or ...
enough
except
far from

for
forward
from
here
how
if
in
in front of
inside
instead of
less
like
more
much
neither ... nor ...
never
no
nobody
nothing
now
of
often
on
once

opposite
outside
perhaps
quickly
slowly
soon
still
then
there
to
too
towards
under
until
well
when
where
why
with
within
without
yes

VOCABULARY BY THEME

QUALITIES

able
acid
angry
automatic
awake
bad
beautiful
bent
bitter
black
blue
boiling
bright
broken
brown
certain
cheap
chemical
chief
clean
clear
cold
common
complete
complex
conscious
cruel
cut
dark

dead
dear
deep
delicate
dependent
different
dirty
dry
early
elastic
electric
equal
false
fat
feeble
female
fertile
first
fixed
flat
foolish
free
frequent
full
future
general
good
great
green

grey
hanging
happy
hard
healthy
high
hollow
ill
important
kind
last
late
left
like
living
long
loose
loud
low
male
married
material
medical
military
mixed
narrow
natural
necessary
new

normal
old
open
opposite
parallel
past
physical
political
poor
possible
present
private
probable
public
quick
quiet
ready
red
regular
responsible
right

rough
round
sad
safe
same
second
secret
separate
serious
sharp
short
shut
simple
slow
small
smooth
soft
solid
special
sticky
stiff

straight
strange
strong
sudden
sweet
tall
thick
thin
tight
tired
true
violent
waiting
warm
wet
white
wide
wise
wrong
yellow
young

PEOPLE

boy
girl
man
woman

in law
10

FAMILY

aunt
brother
cousin
dad
daddy
daughter
father
granddad
grandfather

grandma
grandmother
grandpa
granny
half-brother
half-sister
mother
mum
mummy

niece
nephew
sister
son
step-brother
step-father
step-mother
step-sister
uncle

ANIMALS

alligator
ant
bear
bee
bird
camel
cat
cheetah
chicken
chimpanzee
cow
crocodile
deer
dog
dolphin
duck
eagle
elephant

fish
fly
fox
frog
giraffe
goat
goldfish
hamster
hippopotamus
horse
kangaroo
kitten
lion
lobster
monkey
octopus
owl
panda

pig
puppy
rabbit
rat
scorpion
seal
shark
sheep
snail
snake
spider
squirrel
tiger
turtle
wolf
zebra

NUMBERS

1 one	11 eleven		
2 two	12 twelve		
3 three	13 thirteen	30	thirty
4 four	14 fourteen	40	forty
5 five	15 fifteen	50	fifty
6 six	16 sixteen	60	sixty
7 seven	17 seventeen	70	seventy
8 eight	18 eighteen	80	eighty
9 nine	19 nineteen	90	ninety
10 ten	20 twenty	100	one hundred
	21 twenty-one	1,000	one thousand
	22 twenty-two	10,000	ten thousand
	23 twenty-three	100,000	one hundred thousand
	24 twenty-four	1,000,000	one million
	25 twenty-five		
	26 twenty-six		
	27 twenty-seven		
	28 twenty-eight		
	29 twenty-nine		

TIME

24 hour	12 hour
1	one am
2	two am
3	three am
4	four am
5	five am
6	six am
7	seven am
8	eight am
9	nine am
10	ten am

11	eleven am
12	twelve pm (noon)
13	one pm
14	two pm
15	three pm
16	four pm
17	five pm
18	six pm
19	seven pm
20	eight pm
21	nine pm
22	ten pm
23	eleven pm
24	twelve am (midnight)

DAYS OF THE WEEK

Sunday
Monday
Tuesday
Wednesday
Thursday
Friday
Saturday

MONTHS OF THE YEAR

January	May	September
February	June	October
March	July	November
April	August	December

SEASONS

spring
summer
autumn
winter

COLOURS

black
blue
brown
green

grey
orange
pink
purple

red
white
yellow

COMPASS POINTS

north
south
east
west

DAYS OF CELEBRATION

Boxing Day
Diwali
Easter
Eid al-Fitr
Epiphany
Father's Day

Hallowe'en
Hanukkah
Hogmanay
Mother's Day
Passover
Purim

Rosh Hashanah
Saint Patrick's Day
Shrove Tuesday
Valentine's Day
Veterans Day
Yom Kippur

Vocabulary by Theme

PARTS OF THE BODY

ankle
arm
back
cheek
chest
ear
elbow
eye
face

finger
fingernail
foot
hair
hand
head
knee
leg
lip

mouth
neck
nose
shoulder
stomach
thumb
toe
tooth
wrist

CLOTHING

anorak
apron
baseball cap
bikini
blazer
blouse
boots
bow tie
boxer shorts
bra
cardigan
coat
dress
dressing gown
gloves
hat
high heels
jacket

jeans
jumper
knickers
leather jacket
miniskirt
nightdress
overcoat
pullover
pyjamas
raincoat
sandals
scarf
shirt
shoelace
shoes
shorts
skirt
slippers

socks
stilettos
stockings
suit
sweater
swimming costume
swimming trunks
t-shirt
thong
tie
tights
top
tracksuit
trainers
trousers
underpants
vest
wellington boots

other personal items

belt	handkerchief	purse
bracelet	keyring	ring
comb	keys	sunglasses
cufflinks	lighter	umbrella
earrings	lipstick	walking stick
engagement ring	make-up	wallet
glasses	mirror	watch
hairbrush	necklace	wedding ring
handbag	piercing	

words to do with dressing

button	to get undressed	to take off
to get dressed	to put on	to wear

FOOD
meals

breakfast	lunch	tea
brunch	dinner	supper

words and phrases to do with food

appetite	hungry	sugar
bitter	milk	sugary
fibre	organically grown	sweet
genetically	pescetarian	tasteless
modified	polyunsaturated	thirst
health foods	provisions	thirsty
hunger	snack	to be hungry

Vocabulary by Theme

to be thirsty
to diet
to drink
to gulp
to have a snack

to have a sweet
  tooth
to nourish
to pasteurize
to sip

to slim
vegetarian
vegan

restaurant

bill
dessert
drink
first course

main course
menu
pudding
restaurant

soup
starter
waiter
waitress

dairy

butter
buttermilk
cheese
cream

egg white
eggs
semi-skimmed
  milk

shell
skimmed milk
whole milk
yolk

bread and grains

brown bread
buckwheat
couscous
crumb
crust
grain bread

lentils
loaf
pasta
rice
roll
rye bread

sandwich
sliced bread
toasted sandwich
wheat
white bread
wholemeal bread

fast food

chips
confectionery
crisps
fatty food

fish and chips
French fries
frozen food
hamburger

hot dog
pizza

vegetables, herbs, and beans

artichoke
asparagus
aubergine
avocado
basil
bean sprouts
beetroot
black beans
black-eyed peas
bok choy
borlotti beans
broad beans
broccoli
Brussels sprouts
butter beans
butternut squash
cabbage
carrot
cauliflower
celeriac
celery
chard
chickpeas
chicory

chives
coriander
courgette
cucumber
dill
fennel
garlic
ginger
green beans
kale
kidney beans
leek
lemon grass
lettuce
mangetouts
marjoram
marrow
mung beans
mushrooms
okra
onion
oregano
paprika
parsley

parsnip
peas
pepper
pinto beans
potato
pumpkin
radish
rhubarb
rosemary
runner beans
sage
shallot
soy beans
spinach
spring onion
squash
swede
sweet potato
thyme
tomato
turnip
watercress
yam

fruit

apple
apricot
banana
blackberry
blackcurrant
blueberry
bramble

cherry
clementine
coconut
date
elderberry
fig
gooseberry

grape
grapefruit
guava
honeydew
kiwi fruit
kumquat
lemon

Vocabulary by Theme

lime
lychee
mandarin
mango
melon
nectarine
orange

peach
pear
pineapple
plum
pomegranate
raspberry
redcurrant

satsuma
star fruit
strawberry
tangerine
watermelon

meat

bacon
beef
chicken
duck
goose
halal
ham

lamb
lean
mince
mincemeat
mutton
pork
poultry

rabbit
steak
turkey
veal
venison

cooking

barbecue
bake
chop
fry

grill
roast
slice
steam

stew
stuff

condiments

black pepper
chutney
ketchup
mayonnaise

mustard
olive oil
pickle
relish

salt
table salt
vinegar

drinks

beer	milk	whisky
brandy	mineral water	white wine
cordial	red wine	
juice	spirits	

WORDS TO DO WITH WEATHER

air	freeze	snow
barometer	frost	snowstorm
blizzard	hail	snowy
Celsius	heat	storm
chill	hot	sun
cloud	humidity	sunny
cloudy	hurricane	temperature
cold	ice	thermometer
degree	lightning	thunder
dew	meteorology	thunderstorm
drizzle	moon	tornado
dry	rain	tsunami
Fahrenheit	rainbow	typhoon
flood	rainy	wind
fog	sky	windy
forecast	sleet	

PLACES TO LIVE

apartment	hut	tent
bungalow	igloo	tepee
caravan	mansion	trailer
flat	mobile home	wigwam
house	palace	yurt

Vocabulary by Theme

rooms in a house

attic
basement
bathroom
bedroom
cellar
cupboard
dining room
garage

garden
hall
hallway
kitchen
larder
laundry
living room
nursery

office
pantry
patio
porch
staircase
study

EDUCATION
school words

beaker
binder
blackboard
book
clip
compass
computer
desk
eraser
flask
funnel

globe
glue
laptop
map
marker
paint
paint brushes
palette
pen
pencil
pencil case

pins
protractor
ruler
school bag
scissors
smartboard
stapler
tablet
teacher
test tube

school subjects

Art
Biology
Chemistry
Drama
Economics
Geography

Gym
History
Information
Technology
Languages
Mathematics

Music
Philosophy
Physics
Psychology
Physical
Education

ARTS AND ENTERTAINMENT
arts and crafts

drawing	painting	sculpture
knitting	pottery	sewing

artists and entertainers

actor	conductor	painter
actress	dancer	pianist
artist	director	playwright
audience	drummer	producer
ballerina	guitarist	sculptor
choreographer	magician	singer
cast	musician	vocalist
composer	orchestra	

forms of entertainment

ballet	exhibition	play
concert	film	opera

places of entertainment

art gallery	exhibition centre	stadium
cinema	museum	theatre
concert hall	opera house	

inside a theatre or cinema

aisle	curtain	lighting
box	footlight	microphone
circle	gallery	orchestra pit

row	set	stalls
scenery	speaker	wings
screen	stage	workshop

words to do with entertainment

applaud	conduct	perform
boo	exhibit	play

TRAVEL AND TRANSPORT
types of transport

aeroplane	ferry	ship
bicycle	helicopter	subway
bike	horse	taxi
boat	lorry	train
bus	motorbike	tram
car	plane	tube
coach	scooter	underground

words to do with travel

bus station	rail	taxi
coach station	railway	traffic
crossing	railway station	train
destination	road	travel
journey	route	travel agent
motorway	sail	trip
passenger	sea	tube
port	subway	underground

travelling by air

airport	land	take off
check-in	landing	
fly	plane	

holidays

bed and	hostel	holiday
breakfast	hotel	sightseeing
camp	luggage	suitcase
cruise	motel	tour
excursion	package holiday	tourism
guest house	self-catering	tourist

COUNTRIES AND CONTINENTS
continents

Africa	Asia	South America
Antarctica	Europe	
Australia	North America	

United Nations member states

Afghanistan	Bahrain	Botswana
Albania	Bangladesh	Brazil
Algeria	Barbados	Brunei
Andorra	Belarus	Darussalam
Angola	Belgium	Bulgaria
Antigua and	Belize	Burkina Faso
Barbuda	Benin	Burundi
Argentina	Bhutan	Cambodia
Armenia	Bolivia	Cameroon
Australia	(Plurinational	Canada
Austria	State of)	Cape Verde
Azerbaijan	Bosnia and	Central African
Bahamas	Herzegovina	Republic

Chad
Chile
China
Colombia
Comoros
Congo
Costa Rica
Côte d'Ivoire
Croatia
Cuba
Cyprus
Czech Republic
Democratic
  People's Republic
  of Korea
Democratic
  Republic of the
  Congo
Denmark
Djibouti
Dominica
Dominican
  Republic
Ecuador
Egypt
El Salvador
Equatorial
  Guinea
Eritrea
Estonia
Ethiopia
Fiji
Finland
France

Gabon
Gambia
Georgia
Germany
Ghana
Greece
Grenada
Guatemala
Guinea
Guinea Bissau
Guyana
Haiti
Honduras
Hungary
Iceland
India
Indonesia
Iran (Islamic
  Republic of)
Iraq
Ireland
Israel
Italy
Jamaica
Japan
Jordan
Kazakhstan
Kenya
Kiribati
Kuwait
Kyrgyzstan
Lao People's
  Democratic
  Republic

Latvia
Lebanon
Lesotho
Liberia
Libya
Liechtenstein
Lithuania
Luxembourg
Madagascar
Malawi
Malaysia
Maldives
Mali
Malta
Marshall Islands
Mauritania
Mauritius
Mexico
Micronesia
  (Federated
  States of)
Monaco
Mongolia
Montenegro
Morocco
Mozambique
Myanmar
Namibia
Nauru
Nepal
Netherlands
New Zealand
Nicaragua
Niger

Nigeria
Norway
Oman
Pakistan
Palau
Panama
Papua New
  Guinea
Paraguay
Peru
Philippines
Poland
Portugal
Qatar
Republic of
  Korea
Republic of
  Moldova
Romania
Russian
  Federation
Rwanda
Saint Kitts and
  Nevis
Saint Lucia
Saint Vincent and
  the Grenadines
Samoa
San Marino
Sao Tome and
  Principe
Saudi Arabia
Senegal
Serbia

Seychelles
Sierra Leone
Singapore
Slovakia
Slovenia
Solomon Islands
Somalia
South Africa
South Sudan
Spain
Sri Lanka
Sudan
Suriname
Swaziland
Sweden
Switzerland
Syrian Arab
  Republic
Tajikistan
Thailand
The former
  Yugoslav
  Republic of
  Macedonia
Timor-Leste
Togo
Tonga
Trinidad and
  Tobago
Tunisia
Turkey
Turkmenistan
Tuvalu
Uganda

Ukraine
United Arab
  Emirates
United Kingdom
  of Great Britain
  and Northern
  Ireland
United Republic
  of Tanzania
United States of
  America
Uruguay
Uzbekistan
Vanuatu
Venezuela
  (Bolivarian
  Republic of)
Viet Nam
Yemen
Zambia
Zimbabwe

EXERCISES TO HELP YOURSELF LEARN ENGLISH

Use the following exercises to help you learn English, using the words listed within the book.

ALPHABETICAL ORDER

The words in this book have been listed in alphabetical order:

a,b,c,d,e,f,g,h,i,j,k,l,m,n,o,p,q,r,s,t,u,v,w,x,y,z

Put the following lists of words into alphabetical order, then check your answers and read their meanings in the a–z text of this book.

1	hand foot above below	5	island good wrong allow	9	water kiss heat minute
2	less might flat price	6	apple zero offer fling	10	young university out member
3	previous sale top delicate	7	positive foot respect round		
4	flower rich court fork	8	cough another upper give		

PARTS OF SPEECH AND SENSES

Many words have different meanings and senses, and have different parts of speech. For example, the noun sense of the word *address* can mean 'the place where a person lives or works' and the verb sense that 'you speak to someone'.

Look at the following examples and decide what are the parts of speech of the words in bold. You will find your answers in the a–z text of the book.

1 amount
*The bill **amounts** to three hundred pounds.*   **verb/noun**
*There is a small **amount** of food in the fridge.*   **verb/noun**

2 bank
*I must go to the **bank** to pay a cheque in.*   **verb/noun**
*I **banked** the cheque on Thursday.*   **verb/noun**

3 conduct
*The usher will **conduct** us to our seats.*   **verb/noun**
*His **conduct** on the trip was appalling and he*
   was sent home.   **verb/noun**

4 deal
We are about to sign an important
   *export **deal**.*   **verb/noun**
*I cannot **deal** with this problem just now.*   **verb/noun**

5 edge
*The knife had a very sharp **edge**.*   **verb/noun**
*He **edged** his way towards the front of the line.*   **verb/noun**

Exercises

6 fat

*I used to be quite **fat**, but am now much thinner.*   adjective/noun
*Can you cut the **fat** off the meat?*   adjective/noun

7 green

*She was wearing a **green** dress.*   adjective/noun
*She always wears **green**.*   adjective/noun

8 hand

*I **handed** him the book.*   verb/noun
*My **hands** are very cold after being outside.*   verb/noun

9 increase

*The temperature has **increased** this week.*   verb/noun
*There has been an **increase** in temperature this week.*   verb/noun

10 join

*I'm trying to **join** the two pieces of string.*   verb/noun
*It's impossible to see the **join** in the wallpaper.*   verb/noun

11 kick

*She **kicked** the ball into the net.*   verb/noun
*His leg was injured by a **kick** from a horse.*   verb/noun

12 laugh

*I always **laugh** at his jokes.*   verb/noun
*She heard a loud **laugh** coming from the other room.*   verb/noun

13 middle

*I sat on the **middle** seat in the row.*   adjective/noun
*I was standing in the **middle** of the circle.*   adjective/noun

14 need

*These families are living in **need**.* verb/noun
*They **need** food and warm clothing.* verb/noun

15 oil

*Put more **oil** in the car engine.* verb/noun
*I **oiled** the hinges of the gate.* verb/noun

16 plan

*We need to make **plans** for the future.* verb/noun
*They need to **plan** their future actions.* verb/noun

17 race

*They watched a horse **race**.* verb/noun
*She **raced** to catch the bus.* verb/noun

18 set

*Did you **set** your glasses on the table?* verb/noun
*She was beaten by two **sets** to one.* verb/noun

19 shape

*clouds of different **shapes*** verb/noun
*This early decision **shaped** his career.* verb/noun

20 text

*the **text** of his speech* verb/noun
*She **texted** me about the plans for this weekend.* verb/noun

21 use

***Use** a knife to cut the butter.* verb/noun
*This is only for **use** in emergencies.* verb/noun

22 view

*The **view** from the hill is spectacular.*   **verb/noun**
*I would like to **view** the property.*   **verb/noun**

23 worth

*The painting's **worth** is incalculable.*   **verb/noun**
*The painting was **worth** a lot of money.*   **verb/noun**

Answers:
1 verb, noun; 2 noun, verb; 3 verb, noun; 4 noun, verb; 5 noun, verb; 6 adjective, noun; 7 adjective, noun; 8 verb, noun, verb; 9 verb, noun; 10 verb, noun; 11 verb, noun; 12 verb, noun; 13 adjective, noun; 14 noun, verb; 15 noun, verb; 16 noun, verb; 17 noun, verb; 18 verb, noun; 19 noun, verb; 20 noun, verb; 21 verb, noun; 22 noun, verb; 23 noun, verb.

COLLOCATIONS

Many words in the book are shown with collocations, or other words that they are commonly used with.

Use the entries in the book to decide which of these sentences uses a common collocation.

Which of these sentences is correct?

1
   a _Above all_, we are delighted to be having a baby.
   b _Above much_, we are delighted to be having a baby.

2
   a I'm _no altogether_ pleased about this situation.
   b I'm _not altogether_ pleased about this situation.

3
   a I _backed out_ of the garage.
   b I _backed under_ the garage.

4
   a I find it difficult to _make directions_.
   b I find it difficult to _follow directions_.

5
   a _Pull the kettle off_ for a cup of tea.
   b _Put the kettle on_ for a cup of tea.

6
   a the political party _in office_
   b the political party _under office_

7
   a _Turn through the pages_ of the magazine.
   b _Turn over the pages_ of the magazine.

Exercises

8

  a I _paid for_ my groceries.
  b I _paid_ my groceries.

9

  a I went _shopping_ groceries.
  b I went _shopping for_ groceries.

10

  a I'm _short of_ money just now.
  b I'm _short off_ money just now.

PHRASES

Phrases help us use English in a natural manner. Look at the pairs of phrases below and, checking against the book, decide which one in each pair is correct. You'll find the answers by looking up the relevant words in the book.

1   *a* walk arm in foot
        b walk arm in arm

2   *a* fall asleep
        b stumble asleep

3   *a* bad for you
        b bad off you

4   *a* on business
        b off business

5   *a* cheer up
        b cheer down

6   *a* closed down
        b closed under

7   *a* dress up
        b dress over

8   *a* field trap
        b field trip

9   *a* give something away
        b give something off

Exercises

10.   *a* hand in sock
    → *b* hand in glove

11   → *a* hard of hearing
      b soft of hearing

12   → *a* take something to heart
      b make something to heart

13   — *a* keep your hand in
      b keep your elbow in

14   *a* jump at
  — *b* jump of

15   *a* make open house
  → *b* keep open house

16   — *a* make a point of something
      b do a point of something

17   → *a* run over
      b run under

18   → *a* come to terms
      b go to terms

19   — *a* as well as
      b in well as

20   *a* work someone down
  < *b* work someone up